高等学校试用教材

建筑类专业英语
建筑工程

第一册

卢世伟 孟祥杰		主编
史冰岩 齐秀坤 李 飏		编
李晶纯 南敬石 屠永清 黄 红		
刘建理		主审

中国建筑工业出版社

《建筑类专业英语》编审委员会

总 主 编　徐铁城
总 主 审　杨匡汉
副总主编　（以姓氏笔画为序）
　　　　　王庆昌　乔梦铎　陆铁镛
　　　　　周保强　蔡英俊
编　　委　（以姓氏笔画为序）
　　　　　王久愉　王学玲　王翰邦　卢世伟
　　　　　孙　玮　李明章　朱满才　向小林
　　　　　向　阳　刘文瑛　余曼筠　孟祥杰
　　　　　张少凡　张文洁　张新建　赵三元
　　　　　阎岫峰　傅兴海　褚羞花　蔡慧俭
　　　　　濮宏魁
责任编辑　郦锁林

前　　言

　　经过几十年的探索，外语教学界许多人认为，工科院校外语教学的主要目的应该是："使学生能够利用外语这个工具，通过阅读去获取国外的与本专业有关的科技信息。"这既是我们建设有中国特色的社会主义的客观需要，也是在当前条件下工科院校外语教学可能完成的最高目标。事实上，教学大纲规定要使学生具有"较强"阅读能力，而对其他方面的能力只有"一般"要求，就是这个意思。

　　大学本科的一、二年级，为外语教学的基础阶段。就英语来说，这个阶段要求掌握的词汇量为2400个（去掉遗忘，平均每个课时10个单词）。加上中学阶段已经学会的1600个单词，基础阶段结束时应掌握的词汇量为4000个。仅仅掌握4000个单词，能否看懂专业英文书刊呢？还不能。据统计，掌握4000个单词，阅读一般的英文科技文献，生词量仍将有6%左右，即平均每百词有六个生词，还不能自由阅读。国外的外语教学专家认为，生词量在3%以下，才能不借助词典，自由阅读。此时可以通过上下文的联系，把不认识的生词猜出来，那么，怎么样才能把6%的生词量降低到3%以下呢？自然，需要让学生增加一部分词汇积累。问题是，要增加多少单词？要增加哪一些单词？统计资料表明，在每一个专业的科技文献中，本专业最常用的科技术语大约只有几百个，而且它们在文献中重复出现的频率很高。因此，在已经掌握4000个单词的基础上，在专业阅读阶段中，有针对性地通过大量阅读，扩充大约1000个与本专业密切有关的科技词汇，便可以逐步达到自由阅读本专业科技文献的目的。

　　早在八十年代中期，建设部系统院校外语教学研究会就组织编写了一套《土木建筑系列英语》，分八个专业，共12册。每个专业可选读其中的3、4册。那套教材在有关院校相应的专业使用多年，学生和任课教师反映良好。但是，根据当时的情况，那套教材定的起点较低（1000词起点），已不适合今天学生的情况。为此，在得到建设部人事教育劳动司的大力支持，并征得五个相关专业教学指导委员会同意之后，由建设部系统十几所院校一百余名外语教师和专业课教师按照统一的编写规划和要求，编写了这一套《建筑类专业英语》教材。

　　《建筑类专业英语》是根据国家教委颁发的《大学英语专业阅读阶段教学基本要求》编写的专业阅读教材，按照建筑类院校共同设置的五个较大的专业类别对口编写。五个专业类别为：建筑学与城市规划；建筑工程（即工业与民用建筑）；给水排水与环境保护；暖通、空调与燃气；建筑管理与财务会计。每个专业类别分别编写三册专业英语阅读教材，供该专业类别的学生在修完基础阶段英语后，在第五至第七学期专业阅读阶段使用，每学期一册。

　　上述五种专业英语教材语言规范，题材广泛，覆盖相关专业各自的主要内容：包括专业基础课、专业主干课及主要专业选修课，语言材料的难易度切合学生的实际水平；语汇以大学英语"通用词汇表"的4000个单词为起点，每个专业类别的三册书将增加1000~1200个阅读本专业必需掌握的词汇。本教材重视语言技能训练，突出对阅读、翻译和写作能力的培养，以求达到《大学英语专业阅读阶段教学基本要求》所提出的教学目标："通过指导学生阅读有关专业的英语书刊和文献，使他们进一步提高阅读和翻译科技资料的能力，并能以英语为工具获取专业所需的信息。"

《建筑类专业英语》每册16个单元，每个单元一篇正课文(TEXT)，两篇副课文(Reading Material A & B)，每个单元平均2000个词，三册48个单元，总共约有十万个词，相当于原版书三百多页。要培养较强的阅读能力，读十万个词的文献，是起码的要求。如果专业课教师在第六和第七学期，在学生通过学习本教材已经掌握了数百个专业科技词汇的基础上，配合专业课程的学习，再指定学生看一部分相应的专业英语科技文献，那将会既促进专业课的学习，又提高英语阅读能力，实为两得之举。

本教材不仅适用于在校学生，对于有志提高专业英语阅读能力的建筑行业广大在职工程技术人员，也是一套适用的自学教材。

建设部人事教育劳动司高教处和中国建设教育协会对这套教材的编写自始至终给予关注和支持；中国建筑工业出版社第五编辑室密切配合，参与从制定编写方案到审稿各个阶段的重要会议，给了我们很多帮助。

本书为《建筑类专业英语》建筑工程专业第一册。本册书在编写过程中承蒙哈尔滨建筑大学高伯阳教授、庄重教授、吉林建筑工程学院苗若愚教授、尹德生教授在选材、译文加工等方面给予大力帮助，并提出宝贵意见，谨此致谢。

《建筑类专业英语》是我们编写对口专业阅读教材的又一次尝试，由于编写者水平及经验有限，教材中不妥之处在所难免，敬请广大读者批评指正。

《建筑类专业英语》
编审委员会

Contents

UNIT ONE
Text   Introduction to Mechanics of Materials 1
Reading Material A   Shear Center 6
                B   Allowable Stress Design and Strength Design 8

UNIT TWO
Text   The Tensile Test 11
Reading Material A   Comparative Study of the Mechanical Properties of
                       Ductile and Brittle Materials 16
                B   Strength Theories 18

UNIT THREE
Text   Application of Mechanics of Materials and Its Study Method 21
Reading Material A   Stress 26
                B   Method of Sections 28

UNIT FOUR
Text   Description of the Force and Displacement
         Method 30
Reading Material A   Types of Beams 34
                B   Methods of Joints and Sections for Analyzing a Truss 36

UNIT FIVE
Text   Structure of Buildings 39
Reading Material A   Structural Planning and Design 44
                B   Types of Loads and Types of Stress 45

UNIT SIX
Text   Purpose of Structural Analysis, Modeling of
         Structures and Relation of Analysis and Design 48
Reading Material A   Matrix Analysis of Structures by the Stiffness Method 53
                B   Equilibrium of Single Members 55

UNIT SEVEN
Text   Properties of Concrete and Reinforced Concrete 57
Reading Material A   Property of Structural Steel 62
                B   Nature of Wood and Masonry 63

UNIT EIGHT
Text   Building Code (I) 65
Reading Material A   Building Code (II) 70
                B   Building Code (III) 71

UNIT NINE
- Text　　Early History of Cement and Concrete ... 73
- Reading Material A　The Hydration Reaction ... 78
- 　　　　　　　　　B　Distress and Failure of Concrete ... 79

UNIT TEN
- Text　　Advantages and Disadvantages of Concrete and Its Water-Cement Ratio ... 81
- Reading Material A　Slump Test and Concrete Proportioning ... 85
- 　　　　　　　　　B　Curing Concrete ... 87

UNIT ELEVEN
- Text　　Mortar ... 89
- Reading Material A　Water Retentivity ... 93
- 　　　　　　　　　B　Cement Mortar and Lime Mortar ... 95

UNIT TWELVE
- Text　　General Plannting Considerations ... 97
- Reading Material A　Housing ... 101
- 　　　　　　　　　B　House ... 103

UNIT THIRTEEN
- Text　　Factory Design ... 105
- Reading Material A　Modern Building Construction ... 110
- 　　　　　　　　　B　Building ... 112

UNIT FOURTEEN
- Text　　Fundamental Objective of Structural Dynamics Analysis ... 114
- Reading Material A　Organization of the Text ... 118
- 　　　　　　　　　B　Methods of Discretization ... 120

UNIT FIFTEEN
- Text　　Contents of Theory of Elasticity ... 124
- Reading Material A　Basic Assumptions in Classical Elasticity ... 128
- 　　　　　　　　　B　Members in a State of Two-Dimensional Stress ... 130

UNIT SIXTEEN
- Text　　Historical Development of Finite Element Method ... 132
- Reading Material A　General Description of the Finite Element Method ... 137
- 　　　　　　　　　B　Introduction of Displacement Approach ... 139

- Appendix I　　Vocabulary ... 141
- Appendix II　　Translation for Reference ... 147
- Appendix III　　Key to Exercises ... 167

UNIT ONE

Text　　Introduction to Mechanics of Materials

[1]　Mechanics of materials is a branch of applied mechanics that deals with the behavior of solid bodies subjected to various types of loading. It is a field of study that is known by a variety of names, including "strength of materials" and "mechanics of deformable bodies." The solid bodies considered in this book include axially-loaded bars, shafts, beams, and columns, as well as structures that are assemblies of these components. Usually the objective of our analysis will be the determination of the stresses, strains, and deformations produced by the loads; if these quantities can be found for all values of load up to the failure load, then we will have obtained a complete picture of the mechanical behavior of the body.

[2]　Theoretical analyses and experimental results have equally important roles in the study of mechanics of materials. On many occasions we will make logical derivations to obtain formulas and equations for predicting mechanical behavior, but at the same time we must recognize that these formulas cannot be used in a realistic way unless certain properties of the material are known. These properties are available to us only after suitable experiments have been made in the laboratory. Also, many problems of importance in engineering can not be handled efficiently by theoretical means, and experimental measurements become a practical necessity. The historical development of mechanics of materials is a fascinating blend of both theory and experiment, with experiments pointing the way to useful results in some instances and with theory doing so in others.[①] Such famous men as Leonardo da Vinci (1452—1519) and Galileo Galilei (1564—1642) made experiments to determine the strength of wires, bars, and beams, although they did not develop any adequate theories (by today's standards) to explain their test results. By contrast, the famous mathematician Leonhard Euler (1707—1783) developed the mathematical theory of columns and calculated the critical load of a column in 1744, long before any experimental evidence existed to show the significance of his results. Thus, Euler's theoretical results remained unused for many years, although today they form the basis of column theory.

[3]　The importance of combining theoretical derivations with experimentally determined properties of materials will be evident as we proceed with our study of the subject. In this article we will begin by discussing some fundamental concepts, such as stress and strain, and then we will investigate the behavior of simple structural elements subjected to tension, compression, and shear.

[4]　The concepts of stress and strain can be illustrated in an elementary way by considering the extension of a prismatic bar (see Fig1-1a). A prismatic bar is one that has constant cross section throughout its length and a straight axis. In this illustration the bar is assumed to be loaded at its ends by axial forces P that produce a uniform stretching, or tension, of the bar.

By making an artificial cut (section mm) through the bar at right angle to its axis, we can isolate part of the bar as a free body(Fig. 1-1b). At the right-hand end the tensile force P is applied, and at the other there are forces representing the action of the removed portion of the bar upon the part that remains. These forces will be continuously distributed over the cross section, analogous to the continuous distribution of hydrostatic pressure over a submerged surface. The intensity of force, that is, the force per unit area, is called the stress and is commonly denoted by the Greek letter σ. Assuming that the stress has a uniform distribution over the cross section(see Fig. 1-1b), we can readily see that its resultant is equal to the intensity σ times the cross-sectional area A of the bar. Furthermore, from the equilibrium of the body shown in Fig. 1-1b, we can also see that this resultant must be equal in magnitude and opposite in direction to the force P. Hence, we obtain as the equation for the uniform stress in a prismatic bar. This equation shows that stress has units of force divided by area — for example, pounds per square inch(psi) or kips per square inch(ksi). When the bar is being stretched by the force P, as shown in the figure, the resulting stress is a tensile stress; if the forces are reversed in direction, causing the bar to be compressed, they are called compressive stresses.

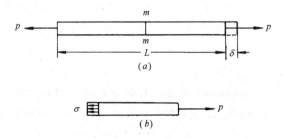

Fig. 1-1   Prismatic bar in tension

$$\sigma = \frac{P}{A} \qquad (1\text{-}1)$$

[5]   A necessary condition for Eq. (1-1) to be valid is that the stress σ must be uniform over the cross section of the bar[2]. This condition will be realized if the axial force P acts through the centroid of the cross section, as can be demonstrated by statics.[3] When the load P does not act at the centroid, bending of the bar will result, and a more complicated analysis is necessary. Throughout this book, however, it is assumed that all axial forces are applied at the centroid of the cross section unless specifically stated to the contrary. Also, unless stated otherwise,[4] it is generally assumed that the weight of the object itself is neglected, as was done when discussing the bar in Fig. 1-1.

[6]   The total elongation of a bar carrying an axial force will be denoted by the Greek letter δ(see Fig. 1-1a), and the elongation per unit length, or strain, is then determined by the equation

$$\epsilon = \frac{\delta}{L} \qquad (1\text{-}2)$$

where L is the total length of the bar. ⑤ Note that the strain $\in$ is a nondimensional quantity. It can be obtained accurately from Eq. (1-2) as long as the strain is uniform throughout the length of the bar. If the bar is in tension, the strain is a tensile strain, representing an elongation or stretching of the material; if the bar is in compression, the strain is a compressive strain, which means that adjacent cross sections of the bar move closer to one another.

New Words and Expressions

(be) subjected to		承受，经受
deformable * [di'fɔːməbl]	a.	可变形的
axially * ['æksiəli]	ad.	轴向地
shaft * [ʃɑːft]	n.	轴，杆状物
derivation * [ˌderi'veiʃən]	n.	推导
realistic * [riə'listik]	a.	现实的，实际的
fascinate * ['fæsineit]	v.	迷住，强烈吸引
blend [blend]	n.	混合，融合
prismatic [priz'mætik]	a.	等截面的
tensile * ['tensail]	a.	拉力的，拉伸的
sectional * ['sekʃənəl]	a.	截面的，部分的
hydrostatic * ['haidrəu'stætik]	a.	静力学的
analogous * [ə'næləgəs]	a.	类似的
analogous to		类似于
submerged [səb'məːdʒd]	a.	浸在水中的
uniform ['juːnifɔːm]	a.	均匀的
denote * [di'nəut]	v.	指示，表示
equilibrium * [ˌiːkwi'libriəm]	n.	平衡
resultant * [ri'zʌltənt]	n.	合力
magnitude ['mægnitjuːd]	n.	大小，尺寸
equation =Eq. [i'kweiʃən]	n.	方程
kip [kip]	n.	千磅
tensile ['tensail]	a.	拉力的
compressive * [kəm'presiv]	a.	压力的，压缩的
centroid ['sentrɔid]	n.	矩心，形心
specifically [spi'sifikəli]	ad.	具体地，特定地
elongation * [ˌiːlɔŋ'geiʃən]	n.	伸长，拉长
nondimensional ['nʌndi'menʃənəl]	a.	无量纲的
adjacent * [ə'dʒeisənt]	a.	相邻的

Notes

① 两个 with 引出各自的独立结构，用 and 连结。doing 是代动词，指 pointing。第二个独立结构的完整形式是 with theory pointing the way to useful results in other instances。

② 从 for 开始是动词不定式的复合结构，作 condition 的后置定语，for 引出动词不定式的逻辑主语 Eq(1-1)。

③ as 是关系代词，引出非限定性定语从句，as 代表整个主句所讲的内容，并在从句中作主语。

④ unless 引出省略的条件句，等于 unless it is stated…。

⑤ where 是关系副词，引导非限定性定语从句。

Exercises

Reading Comprehension

I. Choose the most suitable alternative to complete the following sentences.

1. The objective of our analysis will be the determination of the stresses, strains and deformations produced _____.

   A. with the stretching

   B. in the tension

   C. by the loads

   D. on the equation

2. Galilei made experiments to determine the strength of wires, bars, and beams, although he _____.

   A. advanced a new theory

   B. did not develop any adequate theories

   C. developed any theory of experiments

   D. calculated the critical load

3. A prismatic bar is one that _____.

   A. has constant cross section only

   B. we can isolate part of the bar as a free body

   C. has constant cross section throughout its length and a straight axis

   D. has a straight axis

4. A necessary condition for equation to be valid is that _____.

   A. the experiment must be uniform over the bar

   B. the strain must be uniform throughout the bar

   C. the stress must be uniform over the cross section of the bar

D. the equilibrium must be over the cross section of the bar

5. It can be obtained from Eq. (1-2) as long as _____.

   A. the load is uniform across the whole bar

   B. the distribution has been done throughout the length of the bar

   C. the strain is uniform throughout the length of the bar

   D. the axial force has been done across the whole bar

II. From the list below choose the most appropriate headings for each of the paragraphs in the text, then put the paragraph numbers in the brackets.

   A. The importance of the derivation and experiment   (   )

   B. The illustration of the concepts of stress and strain   (   )

   C. The importance of theoretical analyses and experimental results   (   )

   D. The illustration of useful condition for Eq(1-2) to be valid   (   )

   E. The definition of mechanics of materials and the range of study   (   )

   F. The stress is a necessary condition for Eq. (1-1) to be valid   (   )

III. Complete the following sentences with the information given in the text.

  1. The solid bodies considered in this book include _____ as well as _____.

  2. These properties are _____ only after suitable experiments.

  3. We will begin by discussing some fundamental concepts, such as _____.

  4. This condition will be realized if _____ the centroid of the cross section, as _____.

  5. If the bar is in tension, the strain is _____, if the bar is in compression, the strain is _____.

Vocabulary

I. Choose the word or expression which is the most similar in meaning to the word underlined in the given sentence.

  1. A compressive strain means that <u>adjacent</u> cross sections of the bar move closer to one another.

     A. closing   B. bordering   C. adjoining   D. resembling

  2. In algebra, the sign "X" usually <u>denotes</u> an unknown quantity.

     A. symbolizes   B. indicates   C. expresses   D. implies

  3. These <u>properties</u> are available to us only after suitable experiments have been made in the laboratory.

     A. qualities   B. features   C. quantities   D. attributes

  4. The historical development of mechanics of materials is a <u>fascinating</u> blend of both theory and experiment.

     A. drawing   B. attractive   C. familiar   D. charming

  5. These forces will be <u>analogous</u> to the continuous distribution of hydrostatic pressure over a

submerged surface.

A. alike   B. like   C. similar   D. parallel

II. Match the words in Column A with their corresponding definitions or explanations in Column B.

A	B
1. resultant	a. state of being balanced
2. elongation	b. next(to), lying near(to) but not necessarily touching
3. adjacent	c. deriving or being derived; origin
4. equilibrium	d. as the total outcome of forces or tendencies from different directions
5. derivation	e. the part (of a line etc.) produced by making longer
	f. turn in another direction
	g. statement of how a word was formed and how it changed
	h. must be met with minimum expenditure of a given material

Reading Material A

Shear Center

Consider a beam whose cross section is a channel, Fig. 1-2(a). The walls of this channel are assumed to be so thin that all computations may be based on the dimensions to the center line of the walls. Bending of this channel takes place around the horizontal axis and although this cross section does not have a vertical axis of symmetry, it will be assumed that the bending stresses are given by the usual flexure formula. Assuming further that this channel resists a vertical shear, the bending moments will vary from one section through the beam to another.①

By taking an arbitrary cut as c-c in Fig. 1-2(a), q and τ may be found in the usual manner. Along the horizontal legs of the channel, these quantities vary linearly from the free edge, just as they do for one side of the flange in an I-beam.② The variation of q and τ is parabolic along the web. The variation of these quantities is shown in Fig. 1-2 (b) where they are plotted along the center line of the channel's section.

The average shearing stress $\tau_a/2$ multiplied by the area of the flange gives a force $F_1 = (\tau_a/2)b \cdot t$, and the sum of the vertical shearing stresses over the area of the web is the shear $V = \int_{-h/2}^{+h/2} \tau_t \, dy$. These shearing forces acting in the plane of the cross section are shown in Fig. 1-2(c) and indicate that a force V and a couple $F_1 h$ are developed at the section through the channel.③ Physically there is a tendency for the channel to twist around some longitudinal axis. To prevent twisting and thus maintain the applicability of the initially assumed bending stress distribution, the externally applied forces must be applied in such a manner as to balance the internal couple $F_1 h$. For example, consider the segment of a cantilever beam of negligible weight, to which a vertical force P is applied parallel to the web at a distance e from the web's center line. To maintain this applied force in equilibrium, an equal and opposite shearing force V must be developed in the web.

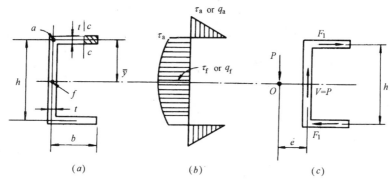

Fig. 1-2 Deriving the location of the shear center for a channel

Likewise, to cause no twisting of the channel, the couple Pe must equal the couple. $F_1 h$. At the same section through the channel, the bending moment PL is resisted by the usual flexural stresses(these are not shown in the figure).

An expression for the distance e, locating the plane in which the force P must be applied so as to cause no twist in the channel, may now be obtained. Thus, remembering that $F_1 h = Pe$ and $P = V$,

$$e = \frac{F_1 h}{p} = \frac{(1/2)\tau_a bth}{p} = \frac{bth VQ}{2p It} = \frac{bth Vbt(h/2)}{2p It} = \frac{b^2 h^2 t}{4I}$$

Note that the distance e is independent of the magnitude of the applied force P, as well as of its location along the beam.④ The distance e is a property of a section and is measured outward from the center of the web to the applied force.

A similar investigation may be made to locate the plane in which the horizontal forces must be applied so as to cause no twist in the channel. However, for the channel considered, by virtue of symmetry, it may be seen that this plane coincides with the neutral plane of the former case. The intersection of these two mutually perpendicular planes with the plane of the cross section locates a point which is called the shear center. The shear center is designated by the letter O in Fig. 1-2(c). The shear center for any cross section lies on a longitudinal line parallel to the axis of the beam. Any transverse force applied through the shear center causes no torsion of the beam.⑤ A detailed investigation of this problem shows that when a member of any cross-sectional area is twisted, the twist takes place around the shear center, which remains fixed. For this reason, the shear center is sometimes called the center of twist.

For cross-sectional areas having one axis of symmetry, the shear center is always located on the axis of symmetry. For those which have two axes of symmetry, the shear center coincides with the centroid of the cross-sectional area. This is the case for the I-beam that was considered in the previous article.

The exact location of the shear center for unsymmetrical cross sections of thick material is difficult to obtain and is known only in a few cases. If the material is thin, as has been assumed in the preceding discussion, relatively simple procedures may always be devised to locate the shear center of the cross section. The usual method consists of determining the shearing forces, as F_1 and V above, at a section, and then finding the location of the external force necessary to keep these forces in equilibrium.

Notes

① 假如槽型截面承受竖向剪力,则弯矩将沿梁的长度方向发生变化。
② 正如工字型截面梁的一个翼缘板,槽型截面梁水平翼缘上的 和 从其自由边开始按直线规律变化。
③ 作用在横截面平面内的各剪力表示在图 1-2(c) 中,在槽型截面产生的一个力 V 和一个力偶 Fh_1 也表示在该图中。
④ 应注意距离 e 与外力的大小及其沿梁长度方向的位置无关。
⑤ 任何通过剪切中心的横向外力不引起梁的扭转。

Reading Material B

Allowable Stress Design and Strength Design

Structural problems are basically of two types: analysis or design. Analysis (sometimes called review) is the process of determining the types and magnitudes of stresses and deformations in a given structure when it is subjected to known or assumed loads. Most of the problems in this chapter have been of the analysis type. The process of design has quite a different goal. In a design situation we are trying to proportion the size and shape of a structure so that it can carry the known or assumed loads in a safe manner.

These two attitudes are not as distinct and separate as they might appear at first glance, because often the design process becomes an analytical trial-and-error procedure in order to determine the "best" size or configuration for a structure. (The phrase "trial and error," while much used and generally understood, can be misleading, as there really is no "error" involved. The writer prefers " trial-and-check " or " select-and-try" as being more descriptive terminology.)

What determines the "best" structure for a given architectural and construction endeavor is quite an impossible question to answer definitively. In pure structural design terms, the word "best" can sometimes be interpreted as "efficiency," that is, efficient use of the material (s) involved through (a) optimum manipulation of the geometry or statics present, and (b) loading the materials with types of stress which they can most easily "take" or resist. Here the word "efficiency" is used, in a narrow sense, to mean just enough material to do the job without waste. Too much material would be "overdesign" and not enough for proper safety would be "underdesign."

As with any type of design, many orders and sequences of compromises are involved and it is a rare (or nonexistent) effort in which the structural, constructional, and functional considerations become coincident. ① The structural design process can never be accomplished in isolation and becomes a mixture of efficiency and compatibility determinations.

There are two different approaches to structural design currently in use. One is called the allowable stress method, in which the structure is shaped and the elements are proportioned so that certain "allowable" stresses are not exceeded. ② (This approach is also referred to as the working stress method or service load method.) These allowable stresses are determined as percentages of the failure strengths of materials under various kinds of stress. For example, the allowable stress in shear for a certain species and grade of wood might be 500kPa, whereas its failure stress in shear might be 1000kPa. The allowable bending stress in structural steel might be determined as two-thirds of its yield value③ (i.e., steel that has a yield strength of 250MPa can be safely stressed to 165MPa). The difference between the two values in each case constitutes a "margin of safety" or factor of safety obtained by dividing the failure stress by the allowable stress. This design method is used for wood structures and for most steel structures. Elements are proportioned so that the computed stresses present under the expected loads (both dead and live) will be less than the allowable stresses. The behavior of the structure under overload or failure load is not considered. Representative allowable stresses for several types of wood are given in Appendix P. Allowable stresses for different steels are given as required in various chapters.

The other approach to design is called strength design, in which the factor of safety is applied in a manner quite different from the allowable stress concept. In the strength design method, various factors of safety are applied directly to the loads which are known or assumed to be acting on the structure. Thus, we conceptually increase the loads that the structure must be proportioned to take by multiplying those loads by specific factors. Such increased or factored loads are called ultimate loads and we then design the member or structure to fail under the application of these increased loads④. (This approach is also called ultimate strength design or ultimate load design.)

Strength design is quite distinct from allowable stress design in that the strength approach proportions a structure to fail under a specified overload and the actual stresses present in the structure under normal loads are not computed. The margin of safety is present in the degree of overload specified. Strength design is widely used for reinforced concrete structures, and overload load factors of 1.4 for dead loads and 1.7 for live loads have been specified by the American Concrete Institute. ⑤

Notes

① 任何设计类型均包含对各种方法和组合的综合考虑,其对结构,施工及功能等因素的选择成为巧合的现象是罕见的,或根本不存在。

② 一种方法叫做容许应力法,这种方法可确定结构的形状,并选择各构件的尺寸,使其不超过所谓的"容许"应力。

③ 在结构钢中弯曲容许应力可以确定为屈服值的三分之二。

④ 这种经过增大或放大的荷载称为极限荷载。我们设计构件或结构,使它们在这种增大的荷载下发生破坏。

⑤ 强度设计被广泛应用于钢筋混凝土结构中,美国混凝土协会规定恒载的超载系数为1.4,而活载的超载系数为1.7。

UNIT TWO

Text   The Tensile Test

[1]   The relationship between stress and strain in a particular material is determined by means of a tensile test. A specimen of the material, usually in the form of a round bar, is placed in a testing machine and subjected to tension. The force on the bar and the elongation of the bar are measured as the load is increased. The stress in the bar is found by dividing the force by the cross-sectional area, and the strain is found by dividing the elongation by the length along which the elongation occurs. In this manner a complete stress-strain diagram can be obtained for the material.

[2]   The typical shape of the stress-strain diagram for structural steel is shown in Fig. 2-1 (a), where the axial strains are plotted on the horizontal axis and the corresponding stresses are given by the ordinates to the curve $OABCDE$. From O to A the stress and strain are directly proportional to one another and the diagram is linear. Beyond point A the linear relationship between stress and strain no longer exists; hence the stress at A is called the proportional limit. For low-carbon (structural) steels, this limit is usually between 30,000 psi, and 36,000 psi, but for high-strength steels it may be much greater. With an increase in loading, the strain increases more rapidly than the stress, until at point B a considerable elongation begins to occur with no appreciable increase in the tensile force. This phenomenon is known as yielding of the material, and the stress at point B is called the yield point or yield stress. In the region BC the material is said to have become plastic, and the bar may actually elongate plastically by an amount which is 10 or 15 times the elongation which occurs up to the proportional limit.① At point C the material begins to strain harden and to offer additional resistance to increase in load. Thus, with further elongation the stress increases, and it reaches its maximum value, or ultimate stress, at point D.② Beyond this point further stretching of the bar is accompanied by a reduction in the load, and fracture of the specimen finally occurs at point E on the diagram.

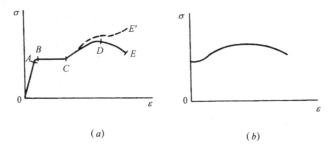

Fig. 2-1   Typical stress-strain curve for structural steel:
(a) pictorial diagram (not to scale); (b) diagram to scale.

[3]   During elongation of the bar a lateral contraction occurs, resulting in a decrease in the

cross-sectional area of the bar. This phenomenon has no effect on the stress-strain diagram up to about point C, but beyond that point the decrease in area will have a noticeable effect upon the calculated value of stress. A pronounced necking of the bar occurs (see Fig. 2-2), and if the actual cross-sectional area at the narrow part of the neck is used in calculating σ, it will be found that the true stress-strain curve follows the ashed line CE'.

Fig. 2-2 Necking of a bar in tension.

Whereas the total load the bar can carry does indeed diminish after the ultimate stress is reached (line DE), this reduction is due to the decrease in area and not to a loss in strength of the material itself.[3] The material actually withstands an increase in stress up to the point of failure. For most practical purposes, however, the conventional stress-strain curve $OABCDE$, based upon the original cross-sectional area of the specimen, provides satisfactory in formation for design purposes.

[4]　The diagram in Fig. 2-1(a) has been drawn to show the general characteristics of the stress-strain curve for steel, but its proportions are not realistic because, as already mentioned, the strain which occurs from B to C may be 15 times as great as the strain occurring from O to A.[4] Also, the strains from C to E are even greater than those from B to C. A diagram drawn in proper proportions is shown in Fig. 2-1(b). In this figure the strains from O to A are so small in comparison to the strains from A to E that they cannot be seen, and the linear part of the diagram appears as a vertical line.

[5]　The presence of a pronounced yield point followed by large plastic strains is somewhat unique to steel, which is the most common structural metal in use today. Aluminium alloys exhibit a more gradual transition from the linear to the nonlinear region, as shown by the stress-strain diagram in Fig. 2-3. Both steel and many aluminium alloys will undergo large strains before failure and are therefore classified as ductile. On the other hand, materials that are brittle fail at relatively low values of strain (see Fig. 2-4). Examples include ceramics, cast iron, concrete, certain metallic alloys, and glass.

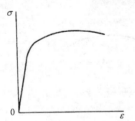
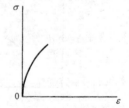

Fig. 2-3 Typical stress-strain curve for structural aluminium alloy

Fig. 2-4 Typical stress-strain curve for a brittle material.

[6]　Diagrams analogous to those in tension may also be obtained for various materials in compression, and such characteristic stresses as the proportional limit, the yield point, and the

ultimate stress can be established. ⑤ For steel it is found that the proportional limit and the yield stress are about the same in both tension and compression. Of course, for many brittle materials the characteristic stresses in compression are much greater than in tension.

New Words and Expressions

cross-section	n.	横截面
plot [plɔt]	vt.	测定,标绘
ordinate ['ɔːdinit]	n.	纵坐标
appreciable [ə'priːʃiəbl]	a.	可估计的,可看到的
elongate ['iːlɔŋgeit]	v.	拉长,伸长
strain harden		应变强化
lateral ['lætərəl]	a.	侧面的
fracture ['fræktʃə]	n.	断裂
whereas * [wɛər'æz]	conj.	而,却,反之
diminish * [di'miniʃ]	v.	减少,缩减
ultimate ['ʌltimit]	a.	极限的,最后的
transition [træn'siʒən]	n.	转变,过渡
linear * ['liniə]	a.	直线的
nonlinear * ['nʌn'liniə]	a.	非线性的
ductile ['dʌktail]	a.	可塑的,延性的
brittle * ['britl]	a.	脆性的
ceramic * [si'ræmik]	n.	陶瓷制品
metallic * [mi'tælik]	a.	金属的

Notes

① …is said to have become plastic 是复合谓语;…actually elongate plastically… actually 和 plastically 均修饰动词 elongate。

② with further elongation the stress increases 中 with further elongation 是倒装,表示强调。or ultimate stress 是同位语。

③ 句中 the bar can carry 做 load 的定语;whereas 引导一个状语从句,表示"反之"、"而"、"却"等之意。

④ 句中 occurring 相当于前面 which occurs,用做定语修饰 strain。

⑤ 句中 analogous to those in tension 做 diagrams 的后置定语。

Exercises

Reading Comprehension

I. Choose the most suitable alternative to complete the following sentences.
   1. A specimen of the material, _____, is placed in a testing machine and subjected to tension.
      A. sometimes in the form of a hard round bar
      B. generally in the form of a round bar
      C. always in the form of an unbreakable bar
      D. seldom in the form of a brittle bar
   2. The force on the bar and the elongation of the bar are measured _____.
      A. when the load is added
      B. as soon as the load is reduced
      C. where the load is increased
      D. once the load is given
   3. The proportional limit of low-carbon is usually between _____.
      A. 3.000psi and 36.000 psi
      B. 30.000 psi and 3.600 psi
      C. 30.000 psi and 36.000 psi
      D. 3.600 psi and 36.000 psi
   4. With an increase in loading, _____, until at point B a considerable elongation begins to occur with no appreciable increase in the tensile force.
      A. the strain increases as rapidly as the stress
      B. the strain increases as fast as the stress
      C. the strain increases more quickly than the stress
      D. the strain increases more slow than the stress
   5. The presence of a pronounced yield point is somewhat unique to steel which is _____.
      A. used in most parts of the world
      B. a commonly used structural metal today
      C. used in any construction
      D. regarded as the only building material

II. From the list below choose the most appropriate headings for each of the paragraphs in the text, then put the paragraph numbers in the brackets.
   A. Further explanation of the strain before fracture occurring   (　　)
   B. A basic concept of the tensile test   (　　)
   C. Introduction of plastic and brittle materials   (　　)

D. The illustration of the proportions to the stress-strain diagram ( )
   E. The relationship between stress and strain ( )
   F. Diagrams analogous to various materials in compression ( )
III. Complete the following sentences with the information given in the text.
   1. The force on the bar and the elongation of the bar _____ as the load is increased.
   2. Thus, with further elongation the stress increases and it reaches its _____, or _____, at point D.
   3. The material actually withstands an increase in _____ to the point of failure.
   4. Both _____ and _____ will undergo large strains before failure and are therefore _____ as ductile.
   5. Diagrams analogous to those in tension may also _____ for various materials _____, and such characteristic stresses as the proportional limit, _____ and the ultimate stress can _____.

Vocabulary

I. Choose one word or expression which is the most similar in meaning to the word underlined in the given sentence.
   1. He collects specimens of all kinds of rocks and minerals.
      A. samples   B. examples   C. speciosity   D. instance
   2. The long war greatly diminished the country's wealth.
      A. narrowed   B. relieved   C. contracted   D. decreased
   3. It is the ultimate point of land before the sea begins.
      A. finishing   B. synthetic   C. last   D. eventual
   4. The soldiers have to withstand hardships.
      A. confront   B. combat   C. oppose   D. gleam
   5. The wages of men averaged $54.54, whereas women's wages averaged but $42.13.
      A. while   B. thus   C. however   D. moreover
II. Match the words in Column A with their corresponding definition or explanations in Column B.

A	B
1. pronounced	a. hard but easily broken
2. stress	b. making longer
3. elongation	c. fact which illustrates or represents a general rule
4. brittle	d. very noticeable
5. ceramics	e. articles made of porcelain, clay, etc.
	f. moving, tending to move, away from the centre or axis

g. tension, force exerted between two bodies that tough, or between two parts of one body

h. strong base of a building, usually below ground-level, on which it is built up

Reading Material A

Comparative Study of the Mechanical Properties of Ductile and Brittle Materials

The main difference between brittle and ductile materials is that the brittle materials break down after a small deformation, whereas the ductile materials ultimately fail only after considerable deformation. ① Therefore, the area under the diagram for ductile materials is considerably greater than that for brittle materials.

The amount of work required to crush ductile materials is greater than that required for brittle materials. Therefore, ductile materials are more suitable for structures designed to absorb the maximum possible kinetic energy of impact without failure.

The brittle materials fail easily under impacts just because their specific work of deformation is very small. Due to their small deformation up to stresses close to the ultimate strength, the same brittle materials are sometimes capable of bearing far greater stresses than the ductile materials provided deformation is under the action of a placid, gradually increasing compressive force. ②

The second distinguishing feature between these materials is that in the initial stages of deformation, the ductile materials may be considered to behave identically under tension and compression. The resistance of an overwhelming majority of the brittle materials to tension is considerably lower than their resistance to compression. This restricts the field of application of brittle materials or requires that special measures be taken to ensure their safe working under tension as, for example, in reinforcement of concrete elements, working under tension, with steel.

A sharp difference is observed in the behaviour of ductile and brittle materials with respect to the so-called local stresses, which are distributed over a comparatively small portion of the cross section of the element but the magnitude of which exceeds the average or nominal value, calculated from common formulas. ③

Since we do not observe any considerable deformation in brittle materials almost up to the moment of failure, the non-uniform stress distribution shown above remains unchanged under tension as well as compression right until the ultimate strength is reached. Due to this, a weakened bar of brittle material with local stresses will fail or crack at a much lower value of the average normal stress $\sigma = \dfrac{P}{A}$ as compared to a similar bar without local stresses. Thus, we may say that local stresses greatly reduce the strength of brittle materials.

The ductile materials are affected by local stresses to a much lower degree. The role of ductility as regards local stresses is to level them to some extent. ④

We have given a very simplified picture of the working of a bar with a non-uniform distribution of stresses. Actually, levelling out of stresses is hindered not only by strain hardening, but also by the change in the stressed state at the location of stress concentration, its transition from a linear stressed state to a three-dimensional stressed state. ⑤

There is one more factor which stipulates the selection of one or the other type of material for practical purposes. Often, while assembling a structure, it is necessary to bend or to straighten a bent element. Since the brittle materials are capable of withstanding only very small deformations, such operations on them usually give rise to cracks. The ductile materials capable of taking considerable deformations without rupture, can be bent and straightened without any difficulty.

Thus, brittle materials have poor resistance to tension and impacts, are very sensitive to local stresses and cannot bear change in the shape of elements made from them.

The ductile materials are free from these drawbacks; therefore ductility is one of the most important and desirable property in materials.

The points in favour of brittle materials are that they are usually cheaper and often have a high ultimate strength under compression; this property may be utilized for work under placid loading.

Thus, we see that ductile and brittle materials have exceedingly different and contrasting properties as far as their strength under tension and compression is concerned. However, this difference in properties is only relative. A brittle material may acquire the properties of a ductile materials, and vice versa. Both brittleness and ductility depend upon the treatment of the material, stressed state and temperature. Stone, which is conventionally a brittle material under compression, may be made to deform like a ductile material; in some experiments this was achieved by pressing a cylindrical specimen not only at its faces but also on its side surface. On the other hand, mild steel, conventionally a ductile material, may under certain conditions, e. g. low temperature, behave exactly like a brittle material.

Hence the properties "brittleness" and "ductility", which we assign to a material on the basis of compression and tension tests, are related to the materials bahaviour only at ordinary temperatures and for the given kinds of deformation. In general, a brittle material may change into a ductile material, and vice versa. ⑥ Hence it would be more precise to speak not of "brittle" and "ductile" materials but of brittle and plastic states of materials.

It must be noted that a comparatively small increase in the ductility of a brittle material (even up to 2 ％ relative elongation before breakdown) enables its use in a number of cases which are otherwise precluded for brittle materials (in machine parts). ⑦ Therefore, research work on improving the ductility of brittle materials such as concrete and cast iron demands the maximum possible attention.

Notes

① 脆性材料与塑性材料的主要区别是脆性材料经过很小变形就能破坏，而塑性材料经过明显的变形才能最终导致破坏。
② 由于脆性材料的应力在接近强度极限以前变形很小，只要压力均匀地逐渐增加，有时脆性材料比塑性材料能承受更大的应力。
③ 我们观察到塑性材料和脆性材料性能的一个最突出的区别是关于局部应力，这些局部应力分布范围只占构件横截面的相当小的一部分，但应力值却超过按通常公式计算出来的平均值或名义值。
④ 局部应力方面的塑性作用在某种程度上使局部应力均匀分布。
⑤ 确切地讲，应力的均匀分布过程不仅受到应变强化的阻碍，而且也受到在应力集中区域应力状态改变的阻碍。这种应力状态的转变是从单向应力状态到三向应力状态变化的。
⑥ 一般地讲，一种脆性材料可以变成塑性材料，反之亦然。
⑦ 我们必须注意到脆性材料塑性的较小的增加（甚至破坏之前的相对伸长达到 2%）就可使它应用在许多原来脆性材料不能应用的地方。

Reading Material B

Strength Theories

As has been already stated, in the case of uniaxial loading it is not difficult to find the breakdown stress which is used as a basis for designating permissible stresses.

It is much more difficult to find the breakdown stress in compound stressed state which is in general characterized by the three different principal stresses. Experiments show that the breakdown state of an element of structure (yield, rupture) depends upon the nature of stressed state, i.e. upon the ratio between the three principal stresses. Since the number of various possible ratios between the principal stresses is infinitely large, there exist a corresponding infinite number of potential states of failure of the structure element. Hence, for each new ratio between the principal stresses it is necessary to experimentally find the permissible stresses anew. It should be borne in mind that it is much more difficult to conduct tests in compound stressed state as compared to simple tension or compression; these tests are more time consuming and expensive, and, as a rule, require special accessories to the machines available in laboratories.[①]

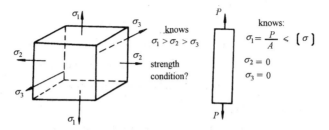

Fig. 2-5

Therefore, it is necessary to find ways of expressing the strength condition under compound stress in terms of σ_y and σ_u obtained from experiments for the uniaxial stress.

Thus, in the general case, when all the three principal stresses are nonzero, the strength of the material is tested according to the following plan:

(1) the three principal stresses $\sigma_1 > \sigma_2 > \sigma_3$ are calculated;

(2) the material is selected;

(3) the critical stresses $\sigma^0 = \sigma_y$ or $\sigma^0 = \sigma_u$ and the permissible stresses are determined experimentally for the given material under simple tension or compression.

It is required to write down the strength condition for the compound stress knowing σ_1, σ_2, and σ_3 and retaining the same safety factor k (Fig. 2-5).

The above problem can be solved only on the basis of the assumption (hypothesis) about the type of function relating the strength of material to the value and sign of the principal stresses, and the factor that causes the critical state.

These factors may be numerous. As a matter of fact, even in simple tension of a bar of ductile material we may put the question: what is the cause of yielding?[②]

We may assume that yielding starts when the maximum normal stresses in the bar reach the yield point σ_y. However, one may as well look at the problem from a different point of view and assume that yielding starts when the maximum elongation of the material reaches a certain limit. One may also assume that large plastic deformations begin to occur when the maximum shearing stresses achieve a certain value.

Thus, we can put forward a number of hypotheses and on their basis formulate various of theories of strength.[③] We shall see later that in simple tension or compression (in uniaxial stress) the results obtained by the strength tests are the same irrespective of the hypothesis used. This is so because the strength test is based directly upon experimental data.

The matters will be very much different in compound stress. In the succeeding sections we shall show how the strength condition changes depending upon the accepted theory. One or the other theory is selected for practical application only after it has been experimentally verified for the compound stressed state.

Whichever strength hypothesis we choose, it can be expressed analytically as some function of principal stresses.

$$\Phi(\sigma_1, \sigma_2, \sigma_3) = \text{const} = C \tag{2.1}$$

In this form the strength theory expresses the condition of constancy (irrespective of the nature of stressed state) of the set of principal stresses that has one or the other physical interpretation. At the same time, equation (2.1) also describes some limiting surface in three dimensional space of the principal stresses. Thus, for example, if $C=\sigma_y$ or $C=\sigma_u$, the corresponding limiting surface is the surface which determines the conditions under which yielding or failure of material takes place.

Before we begin to expound various theories of strength, let us take note that the critical state for ductile materials (appearance of large plastic deformations) as well as brittle materials (appearance of cracks) lies at the boundary of application of Hooke's law (with known approximation sufficient for practical purposes). This enables us to use the formulas which have been derived in the preceding sections and which are valid only within the limits of application of Hooke's law for calculations relating to the strength test.

Notes

① 必须记住，与简单拉伸或压缩试验相比，复杂应力状态下的试验要困难得多。这些试验要花费更多的时间和更高的费用，而且按照规定，在实验室的试验机上要求配置特殊的辅助设备。

② 事实上，即使对塑性材料杆件的简单拉伸情况，我们也可以提出"产生屈服的原因是什么"这样的问题。

③ 于是，我们可以提出一些假设，并以这些假设为基础导出各种强度理论。

UNIT THREE

Text Application of Mechanics of Materials and Its Study Method

[1]   In all engineering construction the component parts of a structure must be assigned definite physical sizes. Such parts must be properly proportioned to resist the actual or probable forces that may be imposed upon them. Thus, the walls of a pressure vessel must be of adequate strength to withstand the internal pressure; the floors of a building must be sufficiently strong for their intended purpose; the shaft of a machine must be of adequate size to carry the required torque; a wing of an airplane must safely withstand the aerodynamic loads which may come upon it in flight or landing. Likewise, the parts of a composite structure must be rigid enough so as not to deflect or "sag" excessively when in operation under the imposed loads. A floor of a building may be strong enough but yet may deflect excessively, which in some instances may cause misalignment of manufacturing equipment, or in other cases result in the cracking of a plaster ceiling attached underneath.① Also a member may be so thin or slender that, upon being subjected to compressive loading, it will collapse through buckling;② i.e., the initial configuration of a member may become unstable. Ability to determine the maximum load that a slender column can carry before buckling occurs, or determination of the safe level of vacuum that can be maintained by a vessel is of great practical importance.

[2]   In engineering practice, such requirements must be met with minimum expenditure of a given material. Aside from cost, at times--as in the design of satellites—the feasibility and success of the whole mission may depend on the weight of a package. The subject of mechanics of materials, or the strength of materials, as it has been traditionally called in the past, involves analytical methods for determining the strength, stiffness (deformation characteristics), and stability of the various load-carrying members. Alternately, the subject may be termed the mechanics of solid deformable bodies.③

[3]   Mechanics of materials is a fairly old subject, generally dated from the work of Galileo in the early part of the seventeenth century. Prior to his investigations into the behavior of solid bodies under loads, constructors followed precedents and empirical rules. Galileo was the first to attempt to explain the behavior of some of the members under load on a rational basis. He studied members in tension and compression, and notably beams used in the construction of hulls of ships for the Italian navy. Of course much progress has been made since that time, but it must be noted in passing that much is owed in the development of this subject to the French investigators, among whom a group of outstanding men such as Coulomb, Poisson, Navier, St. Venant, and Cauchy, who worked at the break of the nineteenth century, has left an indelible impression on this subject.

[4]   The subject of mechanics of materials cuts broadly across all branches of the engineering

profession with remarkably many applications. Its methods are needed by designers of offshore structures; by civil engineers in the design of bridges and buildings; by mining engineers and architectural engineers, each of whom is interested in structures; by nuclear engineers in the design of reactor components; by mechanical and chemical engineers, who rely upon the methods of this subject for the design of machinery and pressure vessels; by metallurgists, who need the fundamental concepts of this subject in order to understand how to improve existing materials further; finally, by electrical engineers, who need the methods of this subject because of the importance of the mechanical engineering phases of many portions of electrical equipment. Mechanics of materials has characteristic methods all its own. It is a definite discipline and one of the most fundamental subjects of an engineering curriculum, standing alongside such other basic subjects as fluid mechanics, thermodynamics, and basic electricity.

[5]　The behavior of a member subjected to forces depends not only on the fundamental laws of Newtonian mechanics that govern the equilibrium of the forces but also on the physical characteristics of the materials of which the member is fabricated. The necessary information regarding the latter comes from the laboratory where materials are subjected to the action of accurately known forces and the behavior of test specimens is observed with particular regard to such phenomena as the occurrence of breaks, deformations, etc. Determination of such phenomena is a vital part of the subject, but this branch of the subject is left to other books. Here the end results of such investigations are of interest, and this course is concerned with the analytical or mathematical part of the subject in contradistinction to experimentation.④ For the above reasons, it is seen that mechanics of materials is a blended science of experiment and Newtonian postulates of analytical mechanics. From the latter is borrowed the branch of the science called statics, a subject with which the reader of this book is presumed to be familiar, and on which the subject of this book primarily depends.

[6]　This text will be limited to the simple topics of the subject. In spite of the relative simplicity of the methods employed here, however, the resulting techniques are unusually useful as they do apply to a vast number of technically important problems.

[7]　The subject matter can be mastered best by solving numerous problems. The number of formulas necessary for the analysis and design of structural and machine members by the methods of mechanics of materials is remarkably small; however, throughout this study the student must develop an ability to visualize a problem and the nature of the quantities being computed. Complete, carefully drawn diagrammatic sketches of problems to be solved will pay large dividends in a quicker and more complete mastery of this subject.

New Words and Expressions

torque * [tɔːk]	n.	扭矩,转矩
composite ['kɔmpəzit]	a.	合成的
aerodynamic [ˌɛərəudai'næmik]	a.	空气动力学的

deflect * [di'flekt]	v.	(使)偏斜,偏转
sag [sæg]	v.	下垂,弯曲
misalignment ['misə'lainmənt]	n.	误差,未校准
plaster ['plɑːstə]	n.	墁灰,灰泥
buckling * ['bukliŋ]	n.	屈曲
configuration * [kənˌfigju'reiʃən]	n.	构件,构造,形状,廓轮
feasibility [ˌfiːzə'biliti]	n.	可行性
expenditure * [iks'penditʃə]	n.	消耗
alternately [ɔːl'təːnitli]	ad.	另一方面,轮流地
precedent ['presidənt]	n.	先例
empirical=empiric [em'pirikl]	a.	经验的
hull [hʌl]	n.	外壳,船体
rational ['ræʃənl]	a.	合理的
indelible [in'delibl]	a.	不可磨灭的
metallurgist * [me'tælədʒist]	n.	冶金学家
phase [feiz]	n.	方面,步骤
curriculum [kə'rikjuləm]	n.	课程
thermodynamics * [ˈθəːməudai'næmiks]	n.	热力学
fabricate ['fæbrikeit]	v.	制造
contradistinction ['kɔntrədis'tiŋkʃən]	n.	对比
blend [blend]	v.	混合
postulate * ['pɔstjuleit]	v.	公理
visualize * ['vizjuəlaiz]	v.	(使)形象化
diagrammatic [ˌdaiəgrə'mætik]	a.	图解的
dividend ['dividend]	n.	利息,股息

Notes

①句中 which 引出非限定性定语从句,修饰"floor";句中 result in 前省略了 may。in (some) instances /in (other) cases 是介词短语,意为:在……情况下。

②句中 so…that 引出结果状语从句;upon being…是介词短语用做时间状语。

③句中 as 引出的从句作插入语,意思是:"正如……一样"。

④句中 in contradistinction to 是介词短语,意思是:与……相区别,与……截然不同。

Exercises

Reading Comprehension

Ⅰ. Choose the most suitable alternative to complete the following sentences.
   1. In all engineering construction the component parts of a structure must be _____.
      A. eterminded clear physical sizes
      B. approached definite physical sizes
      C. given uncertain sizes
      D. assigned undefined physical sizes
   2. The subject may be termed the mechanics of solid deformable bodies.
      A. The subject may be turned down the mechanics of solid deformable bodies.
      B. People may call the subject the mechanics of solid deformable bodies.
      C. The mechanics of fluid deformable bodies may be termed the subject.
      D. The mechanics of solid unformed bodies may be termed the subject.
   3. Mechanics of materials is _____ and one of the most fundamental subjects.
      A. an uncertain theme
      B. a definite training
      C. a clear subject
      D. a deficient discipline
   4. The necessary information _____ comes from the laboratory.
      A. regarding the laboratory of making up the member
      B. involving the materials of which the member is fabricated
      C. regarding the member fabricated in the laboratory
      D. concerning the physical characteristics of the materials of which the member is made up.
   5. Throughout this study the student must _____ and the nature of the quantities being computed.
      A. obtain an ability to survey the problem
      B. get an ability to solve the problem well
      C. have an ability to make the problem deeply depictive
      D. have visualization of the problem deeply

Ⅱ. From the list below choose the most appropriate headings for each of the paragraphs in the text, then put the paragraph numbers in the brackets.
   A. The mechanics of solid deformable bodies   ( )
   B. Mechanics of materials is a quite old subject   ( )
   C. The importance of determining size of the component parts of a structure ( )
   D. The subject of combination of science experiment and Newtonian postulates

      of analytical mechanics (　　)
  E. Broad applications of the subject of mechanics of materials (　　)
  F. The limitation of this textbook (　　)
  G. The significance of studying mechanics
      of materials (　　)

Ⅲ. Complete the following sentences with the information given in the text.
1. Such parts must be properly proportioned to resist actual or probable force that _____.
2. Aside from cost, at times—_____—_____ and _____ may depend on the weight of a package.
3. They, who worked at _____, have left an _____ on this subject.
4. It is a definite discipline and one of _____ an engineering curriculum.
5. The subject matter can be mastered best by solving _____.

Vocabulary

Ⅰ. Choose one word or expression which is the most similar in meaning to the word underlined in the given sentence.
1. The initial configuration of a member may become unstable.
    A. figure   B. appearance   C. form   D. pattern
2. Such a large piece of work requires the expenditure of much money, time and effort.
    A. expenses   B. exhaust   C. waste   D. consumption
3. A floor of a building must be strong enough so as not to deflect excessively excessively.
    A. slope   B. lean   C. slant   D. sheer
4. Mechanics of materials is one of the most fundamental subject of an engineering curriculum.
    A. schoolwork   B. course   C. theme   D. lecture
5. The manager made a rational plan after meeting.
    A. reasonable   B. fit   C. suitable   D. appropriate

Ⅱ. Match the words in Column A with their corresponding definitions or explanations in Column B.

A	B
1. sag	a. to form a mental picture of
2. plaster	b. to bend, hang or sink in the centre as a result of weight or pressure.
3. configuration	c. hang down unevenly; hang sideways
4. visualize	d. soft mixture of lime, sand, water, etc, used for coating walls and ceilings.

5. buckling

e. living organism which is not an animal

f. the assemblage of relative position of the parts of a material system, which may be represented in models plans or diagram.

g. way in which sth. is formed; structure.

h. course taken by a moving person or thing; point towards which a person or thing looks or faces.

Reading Material A

Stress

In general, the internal forces acting on infinitesimal areas of a cut may be of varying magnitudes and directions. These internal forces are vectorial in nature and maintain in equilibrium the externally applied forces. In mechanics of materials it is particularly significant to determine the intensity of these forces on the various portions of the cut, as resistance to deformation and the capacity of materials to resist forces depend on these intensities. ①In general, these intensities of force acting on infinitesimal areas of the cut vary from point to point, and, in general, they are inclined with respect to the plane of the cut. ② In engineering practice it is customary to resolve this intensity of force perpendicular and parallel to the section investigated. Such resolution of the intensity of a force on an infinitesimal area is shown in Fig. 3-1. The intensity of the force perpendicular or normal to the section is called the normal stress at a point. ③ In this book it will be designated by the Greek letter σ(sigma). As a particular stress generally holds true only at a point, it is defined mathematically as

$$\sigma = \lim_{\Delta A \to 0} \frac{\Delta F}{\Delta A}$$

where F is a force acting normal to the cut, while A is the corresponding area. It is customary to refer to the normal stresses that cause traction or tension on the surface of a cut as tensile stresses. On the other hand, those that are pushing against the cut are compressive stresses.

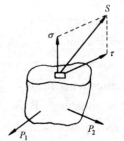

Fig. 3-1 The normal and shearing components of stress

The other component of the intensity of force acts parallel to the plane of the elementary area, as in Fig. 3-1. This component of the intensity of force is called the shearing stress. It will be designated by the Greek letter τ (tau). Mathematically it is defined as

$$\tau = \lim_{\Delta A \to 0} \frac{\Delta V}{\Delta A}$$

where A represents area, and V is the component of the force parallel to the cut. It should be noted that these definitions of stresses at a point involve the concept of letting $\Delta A \to O$ and may be questionable from a strictly atomic view of matter. However, the homogeneous model implied by these equations has been a good approximation to inhomogenous matter on the macroscopic level. Therefore, this so-called phenomenological approach is used.

The student should form a clear mental picture of the stresses called normal and those called shearing. To repeat, normal stresses result from force components perpendicular to the plane of the cut, while shearing stresses result from components parallel to the plane of the cut.

It is seen from the above definitions of normal and shearing stresses that, since they represent the intensity of force on an area, stresses are measured in units of force divided by units of area. Since a force is a vector and an area is a scalar, their ratio, which represents the component of stress in a given direction, is a vectorial quantity.

It should be noted that stresses multiplied by the respective areas on which they act give forces, and it is the sum of these forces at an imaginary cut that keeps a body in equilibrium.

A metric system of units, referred to as the International System of Units and abbreviated SI, from the French Systeme International d'Unites, is used in this text. A change to this modernized metric system of measurement is taking place throughout the world. In the United States a number of major industries have announced plans to convert to SI units. Among these are the automotive, agricultural equipment, and business machine industries. These changes make it inevitable that SI units will become the predominant system of measurement in the United States.

The base units in the SI are meter or metre(m) for length, kilogram(kg) for mass, and second(s) for time. The derived unit for area is a square meter(m^2), and for acceleration a meter per second squared(m/s^2). The unit of force is defined as a unit mass subjected to a unit acceleration, i.e., kilogrammeter per second squared(kg·m/s^2), and is designated a newton(N). The unit of stress is the newton per square meter(N/m^2), also designated a pascal(Pa). Multiple and submultiple prefixes representing steps of 1000 are recommended. For example, force can be shown in millinewtons(1mN=0.001N), newtons, or kilonewtons(1kN=1000 N), length in millimeters (1mm=0.001m), meters, or kilometers(1km=1000m), stresses in kilopascals(1kPa=10^6Pa), megapascals(1MPa=10^6Pa), gigapascals(1 GPa=10^9Pa), etc.

The stress expressed numerically in units of N/m^2 may appear to be unusually small to those accustomed to the English system of units. This is because the force of one newton is small in relation to a pound-force, and a square meter is associated with a much larger area than one square inch[④]. Therefore, it may be more acceptable to think in terms of a force of one Newton acting on one square millimeter. This leads to the notation N/mm^2, a notation which initially was not recommended. However, since this is precisely equivalent to the megapascal(MPa), it is gaining wide acceptance.

Notes

① 在材料力学中,确定各截面上这些力的集度特别有意义,材料抵抗变形和外力的能力都依赖于这些集度。
② 一般来讲,作用在截面微小面积上的力的集度各点不同,它们向截面所在平面倾斜。
③ 垂直于或正交于截面方向的力的集度称为该点的正应力。
④ 这是由于一个牛顿的力与一磅的力相比要小,而一平方米又具有远大于一平方英寸的面积。

Reading Material B

Method of Sections

One of the main problems of mechanics of materials is the investigation of the internal resistance of a body, that is, the nature of forces set up within a body to balance the effect of the externally applied forces. For this purpose, a uniform method of approach is employed. A complete diagrammatic sketch of the member to be investigated is prepared, on which all of the external forces acting on a body are shown at their respective points of application.① Such a sketch is called a free-body diagram. All forces acting on a body, including the reactive forces caused by the supports and the weight of the body itself, are considered external forces. Moreover, since a stable body at rest is in equilibrium, the forces acting on it satisfy the equations of static equilibrium. Thus, if the forces acting on a body such as shown Fig 3-2 (a) satisfy the equations of static equilibrium and are all shown acting on it, the sketch represents a freebody diagram. Next, since a determination of the internal forces caused by the external ones is one of the principal concerns of this subject, an arbitrary section is passed through the body, completely separating it into two parts. The result of such a process can be seen in Fig. 3-2(b) and (c) where an arbitrary plane ABCD separates the original solid body of Fig. 3-2(a) into two distinct parts. This process will be referred to as the method of sections.② Then, if the body as a whole is in equilibrium, any part of it must also be in equilibrium. For such parts of a body, however, some of the forces necessary to maintain equilibrium must act at the cut section. These considerations lead to the following fundamental conclusion:
the externally applied forces to one side of an arbitrary cut must be balanced by the internal forces developed at the cut, or briefly, the external forces are balanced by the internal forces. Later it will be seen that the cutting planes will be oriented in a particular direction to fit special requirements. However, the above concept will be relied upon as a first step in solving all problems where internal forces are being investigated.

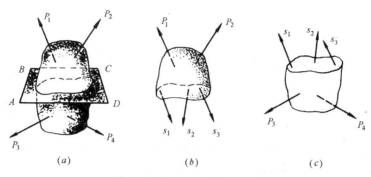

Fig. 3-2　Sectioning of a body

In discussing the method of sections, it is significant to note that some bodies, although not in static equilibrium, may be in dynamic equilibrium.[③] These problems can be reduced to problems of static equilibrium. First, the acceleration of the part in question is computed, then it is multiplied by the mass of the body, giving a force $F=ma$. If the force so computed is applied to the body at its mass center in a direction opposite to the acceleration, the dynamic problem is reduced to one of statics. This is the so-called d'Alembert principle. With this point of view, all bodies can be thought of as being instantaneously in a state of static equilibrium. Hence for any body, whether in static or dynamic equilibrium, a free-body diagram can be prepared on which the necessary forces to maintain the body as a whole in equilibrium can be shown. From then on the problem is the same as discussed above.

Notes

① 对于所考虑的物体，画出完整的示意图，在图中全部外力分别表示在它们的作用点处。
② 这个方法称为截面法。
③ 在讨论截面法时，注意到有些物体虽然并不处于静平衡状态而是处于动平衡状态是有意义的。

UNIT FOUR

Text   Description of the Force and Displacement Method

Description of the Force Method

[1]   1. First of all, the degree of statical indeterminacy is determined. A number of releases equal to the degree of indeterminacy is now introduced, each release being made by the removal of an external or an internal force.①The releases must be chosen so that the remaining structure is stable and statically determinate. However in some cases the number of releases can be less than the degree of indeterminacy, provided the remaining statically indeterminate structure is so simple that it can be readily analyzed. In all cases, the released forces, which are also called redundant forces, should be carefully chosen so that the released structure is easy to analyze.

[2]   2. The releases introduce inconsistencies in displacements, and as a second step these inconsistencies or "errors" in the released structure are determined. In other words, we calculate the magnitude of the "errors" in the displacements corresponding to the redundant forces. These displacements may be due to external applied loads, settlement of supports, or temperature variation.

[3]   3. The third step consists of a determination of the displacements in the released structure due to unit values of the redundants. These displacements are required at the same location and in the same direction as the error in displacements determined in step 2.

[4]   4. The values of the redundant forces necessary to eliminate the errors in the displacements are now determined. This requires the writing of superposition equations in which the effects of the separate redundants are added to the displacements of the released structure.

[5]   5. Hence, we find the forces on the original indeterminate structure: they are the sum of the correction forces (redundants) and forces on the released structure.

Description of the Displacement Method

[6]   The mathematical formulation of the displacement and force methods is similar, but from the point of view of economy of effort one or the other method may be preferable.

[7]   The displacement method can be applied to statically determinate or indeterminate structures, but it is more useful in the latter, particularly when the degree of statical indeterminacy is high.

[8]   1. First of all, the degree of kinematic indeterminacy has to be found. A coordinate system is then established to identify the location and direction of the joint displacements. Restraining forces equal in number to the degree of kinematic indeterminacy are introduced at the

coordinates to prevent the displacement of the joints. In some cases, the number of restraints introduced may be smaller than the degree of kinematic indeterminacy, provided that the analysis of the resulting structure is a standard one and is therefore known.②

[9]   We should note that, unlike the force method, the above procedure requires no choice to be made with respect to the restraining forces. This fact favours the use of the displacement method in general computer programs for the analysis of a structure.

[10]   2. The restraining forces are now determined as a sum of the fixed-end forces for the members meeting at a joint. For most practical cases, the fixed-end forces can be calculated with the aid of standard tables.

[11]   We should remember that the restraining forces are those required to prevent the displacement at the coordinates due to all effects, such as external loads, temperature variation or prestrain.③ These effects may be considered separately or may be combined.

[12]   If the analysis is to be performed for the effect of movement of one of the joints in the structure, for example the settlement of a support, the forces at the coordinates required to hold the joint in the displaced position are included in the restraining forces.

[13]   The internal forces in the members are also determined at the required locations with the joints in the restrained position.

[14]   3. The structure is now assumed to be deformed in such a way that a displacement at one of the coordinates equals unity and all the other displacements are zero, and the forces required to hold the structure in this configuration are determined. These forces are applied at the coordinates representing the degrees of freedom. The internal forces at the required locations corresponding to this configuration are determined. The process is repeated for a unit value of displacement at each of the coordinates separately.

[15]   4. The values of the displacements necessary to eliminate the restraining forces introduced in(2) are determined.④ This requires superposition equations in which the effects of separate displacements on the restraining forces are added.

[16]   5. Finally, the forces on the original structure are obtained by adding the forces on the restrained structure to the forces caused by the joint displacements determined in (4).

New Words and Expressions

statical=static ['stætikəl]	a.	静止的,固定的
indeterminate * [ˌindi'tə: minit]	a.	不确定的
indeterminacy [ˌindi'tə:minəsi]	n.	不确定,不明确
redundant * [ri'dʌndənt]	a.	多余的,过剩的
inconsistency [ˌinkən'sistənsi]	n.	不一致性,不相容(性)
displacement * [dis'pleismənt]	n.	位移,转移
determination [diˌtə:mi'neiʃən]	n.	确定,定义
eliminate [i'limineit]	vt.	除去,删去

settlement ['setlmənt]	n.	沉降,沉积
superposition * ['sju:pəpə'ziʃən]	n.	重合,叠加
formulation * [ˌfɔ:mju'leiʃən]	n.	表达,表述
kinematic * [ˌkaini'mætik]	a.	运动的,动力(学)的
coordinate [kəu'ɔ:dinit]	n.	坐标系,一致
fixed-end force		固端力
deform [di'fɔ:m]	v.	(使)变形
prestrain [pri'strein]	n.	预(加)应变(负载),预加载

Notes

① 句中 each release being made by… 为现在分词短语的独立结构形式,用 做方式状语。
② 句中 provided 是连词,相当于 on condition(that) 意为:假若,倘使。常与 that 连用。
③ required… 为过去分词短语,做后置定语,修饰宾语从句中的主语 the restraining forces; due to… 为形容词短语,相当于 because of。
④ 句中 necessary to… 为形容词短语,做后置定语,修饰 the values of the displacements; introdued… 为过去分词短语做 the restraining forces 的后置定语。

Exercises

Reading Comprehension

I. Choose the most suitable alternative to complete the following sentences.

1. The releases must be chosen _____ is stable and statically determinate.

    A. so that the remaining structure

    B. as to that the remaining structure

    C. therefore the retaining structure

    D. so that the retaining structure

2. In some cases, the number of restraints introduced _____.

    A. should be bigger than the extent of kinematic indeterminacy

    B. will be smaller than the degree of kinematic indeterminacy

    C. can be bigger than the extent of kinematic indeterminacy

    D. may be smaller than the degree of kinematic indeterminacy

3. The determination requires the writing of superposition equations _____ are added.

    A. in which the effects of separating displacements about the restrained forces

    B. in which the affecting separate displacements upon the restraining forces

    C. in which the effects of the separate redundants

    D. in which the affecting separating displacements on the restrained forces

4. The internal forces _____ to this configuration are determined.

   A. at the required locations being corresponded

   B. at the required locations corresponding

   C. at the required locations in correspondence

   D. at the required locations correspondent

5. The released forces, _____ should be carefully chosen.

   A. which are called redundant forces

   B. which may be called the remaining forces

   C. which should be described as superfluous forces

   D. which can be named the forces not needed

II. From the list below choose the most appropriate headings for each of the paragraphs in the text, then put the paragraph numbers in the brackets.

   A. The restraining forces determined by the sum of the fixed-end forces   (   )

   B. Determination of the displacements in the released structure   (   )

   C. Determining of the degree of statical indeterminacy   (   )

   D. The releases introducing inconsistencies in displacement   (   )

   E. The degree of kinematic indeterminacy   (   )

   F. Eliminating the errors in the displacements by the values of the redundant forces

   (   )

   G. The correction forces and forces on the released structure   (   )

   H. General computer programs for the analysis of a structure   (   )

   I. Obtaining the forces on the original structure   (   )

   J. Restraining forces for preventing the displacement   (   )

   K. The values of the displacements necessary to eliminate the restraining forces   (   )

   L. The coordinates representing the degrees of freedom   (   )

III. Complete the following sentences with the information given in the text.

   1. _____ the forces on the original structure are obtained _____ to the forces caused by the joint displacements determined in.

   2. The releases introduce inconsistencies in displacements, and _____ are determined.

   3. We should note that, _____, the above procedure requires no choice to be made _____.

   4. A number of releases _____ is now introduced, each release being made by _____.

   5. The process is repeated _____ at each of the coordinates separately.

Vocabulary

I. Choose one word or expression which is the most similar in meaning to the word underlined in the given sentence.

   1. New techniques led to the <u>displacement</u> of the Fine Art tradition.

A. diversion   B. compression   C. replacement   D. reinforcement
2. He continued testing hypotheses and <u>eliminating</u> them.
   A. diminishing   B. completing   C. suspending   D. removing
3. Chemical substances are described as <u>stable</u> when they tend to remain in the same chemical state.
   A. volatile   B. stationary   C. firm   D. compact
4. <u>Redundant</u> forces should be carefully chosen so that the released structure is easy to analyze.
   A. Independent   B. Surplus   C. Correspondent   D. Diffuse
5. The minor characters are <u>deformed</u> by conditions beyond their power to change.
   A. distorted   B. dismissed   C. disfigured   D. disputed

II. Match the words in Column A with their corresponding definitions or explanations in Column B.

A	B
1. equation	a. not fixed; vague or indefinite
2. indeterminate	b. take or put away, get rid of (because unnecessary)
3. force	c. that branch of applied mathematics which studies the way in which velocities and accelerations of various parts of a moving system are related
4. eliminate	d. a dimension or quantity which is taken as a standard of measurement
5. formulation	e. when acting on a body which is free to move, produces an acceleration in the motion of the body, measured by rare of change of momentum of body
	f. exact and clear statement
	g. a statement that two mathematical expressions are equal
	h. the quantity of water, gas etc., move out of a place by an object

Reading Material A

Types of Beams

A bar that is subjected to forces acting transverse to its axis is called a beam. We will consider only a few of the simplest types of beams, such as those shown in Fig. 4-1. In every instance it is assumed that the beam has a plane of symmetry that is parallel to the plane of the figure itself. Thus, the cross section of the beam has a vertical axis of symmetry. Also, it is assumed that the applied loads act in the plane of symmetry, and hence bending of the beam occurs in that plane. Later we will consider a more general kind of bending in which the beam may have an unsymmetrical cross section.

The beam in Fig. 4-1(a), with a pin support at one end and a roller support at the other, is called a simply supported beam, or a simple beam. The essential feature of a simple beam is that both ends of the beam may rotate freely during bending, but they cannot translate in the lateral direction (that is, transverse to the axis). Also, one end of the beam can move freely in the axial direction (that is, horizontally). The supports of a simple beam may sustain vertical reactions acting either upward or downward.

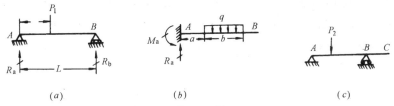

Fig. 4-1　Types of beams.

The beam in Fig. 4-1(b), which is built-in or fixed at one end and free at the other end, is called a cantilever beam. At the fixed support the beam can neither rotate nor translate, while at the free end it may do both. The third example in the figure shows a beam with an overhang. This beam is simply supported at A and B and has a free end at C.

Loads on a beam may be concentrated forces, such as P_1, and P_2 in Fig. 4-1(a) and (c), or distributed loads, such as the load q in Fig. 4-1(b). Distributed loads are characterized by their intensity, which is expressed in units of force per unit distance along the axis of the beam.① For a uniformly distributed load, illustrated in Fig. 4-1(b), the intensity is constant; a varying load, on the other hand, is one in which the intensity varies as a function of distance along the axis of the beam.②

The beams shown in Fig. 4-1 are statically determinate because all their reactions can be determined from equations of static equilibrium. For instance, in the case of the simple beam supporting the load P_1 (Fig. 4-1a), both reactions are vertical, and their magnitudes can be found by summing moments about the ends;③ thus, we find

$$R_a=\frac{P_1(L-a)}{L} \qquad R_b=\frac{P_1 a}{L}$$

The reactions for the beam with an overhang (Fig. 4-1c) can be found in the same manner.

For the cantilever beam (Fig. 4-1b), the action of the applied load q is equilibrated by a vertical force R_a and a couple M_a acting at the fixed support, as shown in the figure. From a summation of forces in the vertical direction, we conclude that

$$R_a=qb$$

and, from a summation of moments about point A, we find

$$R_a=qb\left(a+\frac{b}{2}\right)$$

The reactive moment Ma acts counterclockwise as shown in the figure.

The preceding examples illustrate how the reactions (forces and moments) of statically determinate beams may be calculated by statics. The determination of the reactions for statically indeterminate beams requires a consideration of the bending of the beams and hence this subject will be postponed. ④

The idealized support conditions shown in Fig. 4-1 are encountered only occasionally in practice. As an example, longspan beams in bridges sometimes are constructed with pin and roller supports at the ends. However, in beams of shorter span, there is usually some restraint against horizontal movement of the supports. Under most conditions this restraint has little effect on the action of the beam and can be neglected. However, if the beam is very flexible, and if the horizontal restraints at the ends are very rigid, it may be necessary to consider their effects. To do so requires a statically indeterminate analysis.

Notes

① 集度用沿梁轴线单位长度上的力来表示。
② 沿梁轴线方向长度的函数。
③ 1)both reactions 两端反力；
2)moments about the ends 端点的力矩。
④ 1)statically indeterminate beam 超静定梁；
2)be postponed 留在后面。

Reading Material B

Methods of Joints and Sections for Analyzing a Truss

To design both the members and the connections of a truss, it is first necessary to determine the force developed in each member when the truss is subjected to a given loading. In this regard, two important assumptions will be made:

1. All loadings are applied at the joints. In most situations, such as for bridge and roof trusses, this assumption is true. Frequently in the force analysis the weights of the members are neglected, since the forces supported by the members are usually large in comparison with their weights. ① If the member's weight is to be included in the analysis, it is generally satisfactory to apply it as a vertical force, half of its magnitude applied at each end of the member.

2. The members are joined together by smooth pins. In cases where bolted or welded joint connections are used, this assumption is satisfactory provided the center lines of the joining members are concurrent.

Because of these two assumptions, each truss member acts as a two-force member, and therefore the forces acting at the ends of the member must be directed along the axis of the member. If the force tends to elongate the member, it is a tensile force, whereas if the force tends to shorten the member, it is a compressive force. In the actual design of a truss it is important to state whether the nature of the force is tensile or compressive. Most often, compression members must be made thicker than tension members, because of the buckling or column effect that occurs when a member is in compression.

The following procedure provides a typical means for analyzing a truss using the method of joints.

Draw the free-body diagram of a joint having at least one known force and at most two unknown forces. (If this joint is at one of the supports, it generally will be necessary to know the external reactions at the truss support.) Use one of the two methods described above for establishing the sense of an unknown force. Orient the x and y axes such that the forces on the freebody diagram can be easily resolved into their x and y components and then apply the two force equilibrium equations $\Sigma F_x = 0$ and $\Sigma F_y = 0$. Solve for the two unknown member forces and verify their correct sense.

Continue to analyze each of the other joints, where again it is necessary to choose a joint having at most two unknowns and at least one known force.② In this regard, realize that once the force in a member is found from the analysis of a joint at one of its ends, the result can be used to analyze the forces acting on the joint at its other end. Strict adherence to the principle of action, equal but opposite reaction must, of course, be observed. Remember, a member in compression "pushes" on the joint and a member in tension "pulls" on the joint.

The following procedure provides a means for applying the method of sections to determine the forces in the members of a truss.

Make a decision as to how to "cut" or section the truss through the members where forces are to be determined. Before isolating the appropriate section, it may first be necessary to determine the truss's external reactions, so that the three equilibrium equations are used only to solve for member forces at the cut section. Draw the free-body diagram of that part of the sectioned truss which has the least number of forces acting on it. Use one of the two methods described above for establishing the sense of an unkown member force.

Try to apply the three equations of equilibrium such that simultaneous solution of equations is avoided. In this regard, moments should be summed about a point that lies at the intersection of the lines of action of two unknown forces, so that the third unknown force is determined directly from the moment equation.③ If two of the unknown forces are parallel, forces may be summed perpendicular to the direction of these unknowns to determine directly the third unknown force.

Notes

①在力法中由于作用在构件上的外荷载比构件本身的自重往往大得多，构件的自重常常被忽略掉。

②继续分析其余各结点时，仍有必要选择结点，使该结点最多有两个未知量而且至少有一个已知力。

③在这方面，对于两个未知力作用线交点的各力矩都要相加，这样只通过力矩平衡方程就能确定出第三个未知力。

UNIT FIVE

Text Structure of Buildings

[1]　Considering only the engineering essentials, the structure of a building can be defined as the assemblage of those parts which exist for the purpose of maintaining shape and stability.① Its primary purpose is to resist any loads applied to the building and to transmit those to the ground.

[2]　In terms of architecture, the structure of a building is and does much more than that. It is an inseparable part of the building form and to varying degrees is a generator of that form. Used skillfully, the building structure can establish or reinforce orders and rhythms among the architectural volumes and planes. It can be visually dominant or recessive. It can develop harmonies or conflicts. It can be both confining and emancipating. And, unfortunately in some cases, it cannot be ignored. It is physical.

[3]　The structure must also be engineered to maintain the architectural form. The principles and tools of physics and mathematics provide the basis for differentiating between rational and irrational forms in terms of construction. Artists can sometimes generate shapes that obviate any consideration of science, but architects cannot.

[4]　There are at least three items that must be present in the structure of a building:
　　stability
　　strength and stiffness
　　economy

[5]　Taking the first of the three requirements, it is obvious that stability is needed to maintain shape. An unstable building structure implies unbalanced forces or a lack of equilibrium and a consequent acceleration of the structure or its pieces.

[6]　The requirement of strength means that the materials selected to resist the stresses generated by the loads and shapes of the structure(s) must be adequate. Indeed, a "factor of safety" is usually provided so that under the anticipated loads, a given material is not stressed to a level even close to its rupture point. The material property called stiffness is considered with the requirement of strength. Stiffness is different from strength in that it directly involves how much a structure strains or deflects under load.② A material that is very strong but lacking in stiffness will deform too much to be of value in resisting the forces applied.

[7]　Economy of a building structure refers to more than just the cost of the materials used. Construction economy is a complicated subject involving raw materials, fabrication, erection, and maintenance.③ Design and construction labor costs and the costs of energy consumption must be considered. Speed of construction and the cost of money (interest) are also factors. In most design situations, more than one structural material requires consideration. Competitive alternatives almost always exist, and the choice is seldom obvious.

[8] Apart from these three primary requirements, several other factors are worthy of emphasis. First, the structure or structural system must relate to the building's function. It should not be in conflict in terms of form. For example, a linear function demands a linear structure, and therefore it would be improper to roof a bowling alley with a dome. Similarly, a theater must have large, unobstructed spans but a fine restaurant probably should not. Stated simply, the structure must be appropriate to the function it is to shelter. ④

[9] Second, the structure must be fire-resistant. It is obvious that the structural system must be able to maintain its integrity at least until the occupants are safely out. Building codes specify the number of hours for which certain parts of a building must resist the heat without collapse. The structural materials used for those elements must be inherently fire-resistant or be adequately protected by fireproofing materials. The degree of fire resistance to be provided will depend upon a number of items, including the use and occupancy load of the space, its dimensions, and the location of the building. ⑤

[10] Third, the structure should integrate well with the building's circulation systems. It should not be in conflict with the piping systems for water and waste, the ducting systems for air, or (most important) the movement of people. It is obvious that the various building systems must be coordinated as the design progresses. One can design in a sequential step-by-step manner within any one system, but the design of all of them should move in a parallel manner toward completion. Spatially, all the various parts of a building are interdependent.

[11] Fourth, the structure must be psychologically safe as well as physically safe. A high-rise frame that sways considerably in the wind might not actually be dangerous but may make the building uninhabitable just the same. Lightweight floor systems that are too "bouncy" can make the users very uncomfortable. Large glass windows, uninterrupted by dividing mullions, can be quite safe but will appear very insecure to the occupant standing next to one 40 floors above the street.

[12] Sometimes the architect must make deliberate attempts to increase the apparent strength or solidness of the structure. This apparent safety may be more important than honestly expressing the building's structure, because the untrained viewer cannot distinguish between real and perceived safety.

New words and Expressions

assemblage[ə'semblidʒ]	n.	集合,组装
in terms of		从…方面来说
to varying degrees		在不同程度上
irrational[i'ræʃənl]	a.	无理的
dominant * ['dɔminənt]	a.	支配的
recessive[ri'sesiv]	a.	后退的
emancipate[i'mænsipeit]	vt.	使不受…束缚

differentiate * [ˌdifə'renʃieit]	vt.	区分,区别
obviate['ɔbvieit]	vt.	消除,避免
rupture * ['rʌptʃə]	n.	裂开
in that		既然,因为
fabrication * [ˌfæbri'keiʃən]	n.	制作
erection[i'rekʃən]	n.	装配
alternative[ɔːl'təːnətiv]	n.	取舍
unobstructed['ʌnəb'strʌktid]	a.	没有障碍的
competitive * [kəm'petitiv]	a.	竞争的
integrity[in'tegriti]	n.	完整,完全
dome[dəum]	n.	圆屋顶
occupant['ɔkjupənt]	n.	占用者,居住者
inherent[in'hiərənt]	a.	内在的,固有的
integrate['intigreit]	v.	使成整体
circulation[ˌsəːkju'leiʃən]	n.	流线循环,流通
in conflict with		抵触,冲突
spatially * ['speiʃəli]	ad.	空间地
deliberate[di'libərit]	a.	深思熟虑的
bouncy['baunsi]	a.	有弹性的
mullion['mʌliən]	n.	(窗门的)直梃

Notes

① 句中的 considering 是介词,意为:就…而言;be defined as 意为:"定义为……"。
② in that 引导的是原因状语从句;how 引导的是 involves 的宾语从句。
③ complicated 和 involving raw materials 均做 subject 的定语。
④ it is to shelter 做 the function 的定语从句,省略连词 that。
⑤ to be provided 做 fine resistance 的定语;including 相当于非限定性定语从句 which include。

Exercises

Reading Comprehension

Ⅰ. Choose the most suitable alternative to complete the following sentences.
  1. The structure of a building can be defined as the assemblage of those parts which exist _____.
    A. to make the building beautiful

B. to keep the building from falling down

C. for the purpose of assembling as many people as it can

D. for the purpose of maintaining shape and stability

2. The requirement of strength means _____.

   A. that material selected should be strong enough to resist the stress generated by the loads and shapes of the structure must be adequate

   B. that material selected should be hard enough to resist the load

   C. that the building technique should meet the standard of the code

   D. that the workers should work hard in order to complete the project in time.

3. _____ that obviate any consideration of science, but architects cannot.

   A. Scientists sometimes can make shapes

   B. Artists from time to time can produce shapes

   C. Engineers can usually generate shapes

   D. Architectural students can be allowed to produce shapes

4. Construction economy is a complicated subject _____.

   A. which is made up of raw materials, energy consumption and erection

   B. which involves structural material, construction labor and maintenance

   C. which consists of fabrication, the quality of material and the speed of construction

   D. which involves raw materials, erection, fabrication and maintenance

5. Large glass windows of 40 floors above the street, uninterrupted by dividing mullion, can

   A. make the occupant fall down

   B. make the occupants headache

   C. be quite safe

   D. be quite dangerous

Ⅱ. From the list below choose the most appropriate headings for each of the paragraphs in the text, then put the paragraph numbers in the brackets.

   A. The importance of generating form ( )

   B. Fire-resistant material in building ( )

   C. Stability of a building structure ( )

   D. Three items present being in the structure of a building ( )

   E. Several other factors which are necessary to emphasize ( )

   F. Strength of a building structure ( )

   G. The definition of building construction ( )

   H. The deliberation to increase the strength or solidness of the structure ( )

   I. The importance of psychological safety ( )

   J. The difference between the artists and engineers in considering shape ( )

   K. The meaning of economy in building construction ( )

   L. The need in integration ( )

Ⅲ. Complete the following sentences with the information given in the text.

1. Used skillfully, the building structure can _____ or _____ orders and rhythms among the architectural _____ and _____.
2. There are at least three items that must be present in the structure of a building:
   1) _____ 2) _____ 3) _____
3. Construction economy is a complicated subject involving _____, _____, _____ and _____.
4. It should not be in conflict _____ form.
5. The structural materials used for those elements must be _____ fire-resistant or be adequately protected by _____.

Vocabulary

I. Choose one word or expression which is the most similar in meaning to the word underlined in the given sentence.
   1. Efficiency is the <u>dominant</u> idea in many building business.
      A. permanent   B. paramount   C. perceptive   D. pensive
   2. We have just been picturing nature as an <u>assemblage</u> of particles set in a framework of space and time.
      A. a connection   B. a collection   C. a breakage   D. a package
   3. One <u>property</u> of this material is that it can endure much stress.
      A. quality   B. personality   C. capability   D. identity
   4. He <u>emancipated</u> her from superstition(迷信).
      A. participated   B. plunged   C. reinforced   D. liberated
   5. Can you <u>differentiate</u> the works between apartment and flat?
      A. determine   B. diminish   C. distinguish   D. separate

II. Match the words in Column A with their corresponding definitions or explanations in Column B.

A	B
1. mullion	a. tube through which liquids or gases can flow
2. inherent	b. vertical stone division between parts of a window
3. alternative	c. keep or hold, restrict with limits
4. certificate	d. existing as a natural and permanent part or quality of
5. code	e. collection of laws arranged in a system
	f. one of more than two possibilities
	g. written statement, made by sb. in authority, that may be used as proof or evidence of sth
	h. instrument which records the strength, duration and distance away from earthquakes

Reading Material A

Structural Planning and Design

The building designer needs to understand the behavior of physical structures under load. An ability to intuit or "feel" structural behavior is possessed by those having much experience involving structural analysis, both qualitative and quantitative. The consequent knowledge of how forces, stresses, and deformations build up in different materials and shapes is vital to the development of this "sense".

Beginning this study of forces and stresses and deformations is most easily done through quantitative methods. These two subjects form the basis for all structural planning and design and are very difficult to learn in the abstract.

In most building design efforts, the initial structural planning is done by the architect. Ideally, the structural and mechanical consultants should work side by side with the architect from the conception of a project to the final days of construction. In most cases, however, the architect must make some initial assumptions about the relationships to be developed between the building form and the structural system.① A solid background in structural principles and behavior is needed to make these assumptions with any reasonable degree of confidence. The shape of the structural envelope, the location of all major supporting elements, the directionality (if any) of the system, the selection of the major structural materials, and the preliminary determination of span lengths are all part of the structural planning process.

Structural design, on the other hand, is done by both the architect and the engineer. The preliminary determination of the size of major structural elements, providing a check on the rationality of previous assumptions, is done by the architect and/or the engineer.② Final structural design, involving a complete analysis of all the parts and components, the working out of structural details, and the specifying of structural materials and methods of construction is almost always done by the structural engineer.

Of the two areas, structural planning is far more complex than structural design. It involves the previously mentioned "feeling for structure" or intuition that comes through experience. Structural design can be learned from lectures and books, but it is likely that structural planning cannot. Nevertheless, some insight and judgment can be developed from a minimal background in structural analysis and design. If possible, this should be gained from an architectural standpoint, emphasizing the relationship between the quantities and the resulting qualities wherever possible, rather than from an engineering approach.③

This study of quantitative structures can be thorough enough to permit the architect to do completely the analysis for smaller projects, although such depth is not absolutely necessary. At the very least it should provide the knowledge and vocabulary necessary to work with the consulting engineer. It must be remembered that the architect receives much more education that is oriented toward creativity than does the engineer, and therefore needs to maintain control over the design. It is up to the architect to ask intelligent questions and suggest viable alternatives. If handicapped by structural ignorance, some of the design decisions will, in effect, be made by others.

Notes

①然而,在大多数情况下,建筑师必须对建筑形式和结构系统之间的关系做一些初步的设想。
②如果对前面所做假设的合理性进行了核对,那么主要结构构件尺寸的初步确定就可由建筑师或工程师单独完成或共同完成。
③如果可能,结构布置应该从建筑观点特别是从可能定量和定性之间关系中得到而不是从工程方法中获得。

Reading Material B

Types of Loads and Types of Stress

Types of Loads

In general, loads that act on building structures can be divided into two groups: those due to gravitational attraction and those resulting from other natural causes and elements. Gravity loads can be further classified into two groups: live load and dead load.① Building live loads include people and most movable objects within the structure or on top of it. Snow is a live load. So is a grand piano, a safe, or a water bed. Appendix O provides some typically recommended live loads for various types of occupancy within building structures. Research bears out that these figures represent probable maximum values for live loads during the lifetime of a structure. Such loads are seldom realized. What is more likely is an unexpected change in the use of the space. One can sense the problems that might result if an abandoned school is purchased for use as a warehouse (to store bowling balls). Dead loads, on the other hand, generally include the immovable objects in a building. The walls (both interior and exterior), floors, mechanical and electrical equipment, and the structural elements themselves are examples of dead loads.

The snow map of Appendix N gives the maximum snow load that can reasonably be expected in various parts of the United States. Like the live-load values, such large snowfalls seldom occur. Nevertheless, we must design for some level of probability and should not forget such occurrences as the more than-500-millimeter snowfall that hit the southeastern United States in 1974, resulting in many small building failures.

Natural forces not due to gravity that act on buildings are provided by wind and earthquakes. Wind load is a lateral load that varies in intensity with height. (Hurricanes and tornadoes present special design problems, and local building codes often require certain types of resistive construction.) A probable wind pressure map is given in Appendix N.

Earthquakes are also treated as lateral loads (at least for preliminary design purposes), but it is well known that buildings in earthquakes are subjected to vertical forces as well. [2] Design methods are not fully developed for disaster loadings such as tornadoes and earthquakes, and research continues in these areas.

One final type of load is an impact load, usually due to moving equipment, which occurs within or on the structure. Most structural materials can withstand a sudden and temporary load of higher magnitude than a load that is applied slowly. For this reason, the specified permissible stress magnitudes are substantially increased when such loads govern the design. No permanent damage is done by a moderate impact load provided that it does not occur repeatedly. (An earthquake is a good example of a severe and repeating impact load.)

All the tables and maps referred to in this text, as part of the appendices, provide rough data only. The designer should consult local building codes, which always take precedence. The designer also bears the professional responsibility for increasing any recommended design loads when the situation warrants it.

Types of stress

A fundamental concept in the structural analysis of buildings is that objects are in a state of equilibrium. This means there are no unbalanced forces acting on the structure or its parts at any point. All forces counteract one another, and this results in equilibrium. The structural element or object does not accelerate because the net force acting on it is zero, but it does respond to these forces internally. It is pushed or pulled and otherwise deformed, giving off energy as heat as it resists the forces. Internal stresses of varying types and magnitudes accompany the deformations to provide this resistance.

These stresses are named by their action or behavior (i.e., tension, compression, shear, and bending). Tensile and compressive stresses which act through the axis or center of mass of an object are evenly distributed over the resisting area and result in all the material fibers being stressed to like amounts. Shearing stresses and, more important, bending stresses are not uniform and usually result in a few fibers of material being deformed to their limit while others remain unstressed or nearly so. Bending is, by far, the structurally least efficient way to carry loads.

Assuming for the moment that we have a material equally strong in tension, compression, shear, and bending, it would be best to load it in tension to achieve its maximum structural capacity. Compressive forces, if applied to a long slender structure, can cause buckling. Buckling always occurs under less load than would be required to fail the materials in true compression (i. e. , crushing). Of course, materials are not equal in strength when loaded in different ways. ③ Some materials have almost no tensile strength, and generalizations are very difficult to make. As explained in succeeding chapters, shearing stresses will cause tension and compression; and bending is actually a combination of shear, tension, and compression. Because of the previously mentioned uneven distribution of stress intensity, however, bending is always the most damaging load that can be applied to any resisting structural material.

Notes

①自重可以进一步分为活载与恒载两种。
②地震也当作横向荷载处理（起码对初步设计目的来说），但众所周知在发生地震过程中，建筑物同时受到垂直力作用。
③当然，当受到不同方式荷载作用时，材料的强度是不相同的。

UNIT SIX

Text   Purpose of Structural Analysis, Modeling of Structures and Relation of Analysis and Design

[1]   Structural analysis is the process of determining the forces and deformations in structures due to specified loads so that the structure can be designed rationally, and so that the state of safety of existing structures can be checked.①

[2]   In the design of structures, it is necessary to start with a concept leading to a configuration which can then be analyzed. This is done so members can be sized and the needed reinforcing determined, in order to: a) carry the design loads without distress or excessive deformations(serviceability or working condition); and b) to prevent collapse before a specified overload has been placed on the structure (safety or ultimate condition).

[3]   Since normally elastic conditions will prevail under working loads, a structural theory based on the assumptions of elastic behavior is appropriate for determining serviceability conditions. Collapse of a structure will usually occur only long after the elastic range of the materials has been exceeded at critical points, so that an ultimate strength theory based on the inelastic behavior of the materials is necessary for a rational determination of the safety of a structure against collapse. Nevertheless, an elastic theory can be used to determine a safe approximation to the strength of ductile structures(the lower bound approach of plasticity), and this approach is customarily followed in reinforced concrete practice. For this reason only the elastic theory of structures is pursued in this chapter.

[4]   Looked at critically, all structures are assemblies of three-dimensional elements, the exact analysis of which is a forbidding task even under ideal conditions and impossible to contemplate under conditions of professional practice.② For this reason, an important part of the analyst's work is the simplification of the actual structure and loading conditions to a model which is susceptible to rational analysis.

[5]   Thus, a structural framing system is decomposed into a slab and floor beams which in turn frame into girders carried by columns which transmit the loads to the foundations. Since traditional structural analysis has been unable to cope with the action of the slab, this has often been idealized into a system of strips acting as beams. Also, long-hand methods have been unable to cope with three-dimensional framing systems, so that the entire structure has been modeled by a system of planar subassemblies, to be analyzed one at a time. The modern matrix-computer methods have revolutionized structural analysis by making it possible to analyze entire systems, thus leading to more reliable predictions about the behavior of structures under loads.

[6]   Actual loading conditions are also both difficult to determine and to express realistically,

and must be simplified for purposes of analysis. Thus, traffic loads on a bridge structure, which are essentially both of dynamic and random nature, are usually idealized into statically moving standard trucks, or distributed loads, intended to simulate the most severe loading conditions occurring in practice. ③

[7] Similarly, continuous beams are sometimes reduced to simple beams, rigid joints to pin—joints, filler-walls are neglected, shear walls are considered as beams; in deciding how to model a structure so as to make it reasonably realistic but at the same time reasonably simple, the analyst must remember that each such idealization will make the solution more suspect. ④ The more realistic the analysis, the greater will be the confidence which it inspires, and the smaller may be the safety factor (or factor of ignorance). Thus, unless code provisions control, the engineer must evaluate the extra expense of a thorough analysis as compared to possible savings in the structure.

[8] The most important use of structural analysis is as a tool in structural design. As such, it will usually be a part of a trial-and-error procedure, in which an assumed configuration with assumed dead loads is analyzed, and the members designed in accordance with the results of the analysis. ⑤ This phase is called the preliminary design; since this design is still subject to change, usually a crude, fast analysis method is adequate. At this stage, the cost of the structure is estimated, loads and member properties are revised, and the design is checked for possible improvements. The changes are now incorporated in the structure, a more refined analysis is performed, and the member design is revised. This project is carried to convergence, the rapidity of which will depend on the capability of the designer. It is clear that a variety of analysis methods, ranging from 'quick and dirty' to 'exact', is needed for design purposes. ⑥

[9] An efficient analyst must thus be in command of the rigorous methods of analysis, must be able to reduce these to shortcut methods by appropriate assumptions, and must be aware of available design and analysis aids, as well as simplifications permitted by applicable building codes. An up-to-date analyst must likewise be versed in the bases of matrix structural analysis and its use in digital computers as well as in the use of available analysis programs or software.

New Words and Expressions

distress[dis'tres]	n.	损坏
planar['pleinə]	a.	平面的,平的
idealise(-ize)[ai'diəlaiz]	v.	(使)理想化
prevail[pri'veil]	vi.	战胜;占优势
serviceability[ˌsəːvisə'biliti]	n.	功能,耐用性
ultimate['ʌltimit]	n.	极限,终极
	a.	极限的

approximation * [əˌprɔksi'meiʃən]	n.	近似,近似值
plasticity [plæs'tisiti]	n.	可塑性
versed ['və:st]	a.	精通的,熟练的
three-dimensional		三维的
susceptible [sə'septəbl]	a.	易受影响的
decompose [ˌdi:kəm'pəuz]	v.	分解
slab [slæb]	n.	平板,厚板
contemplate ['kɔntempleit]	v.	思考,打算
girder ['gə:də]	n.	桁架,梁
subassembly ['sʌbə'sembli]	n.	组件,部件
matrix-computer method		矩阵计算法
prediction [pri'dikʃən]	n.	预言,预测
random * ['rændəm]	a.	随机的
simulate ['simju:leit]	v.	假装,模拟
code [kəud]	n.	规范,规则
trial-and-error		试算
in accordance with		按照,根据
pin-joint		铰接点
incorporate * [in'kɔ:pəreit]	v.	合并,纳入
convergence * [kən'və:dʒəns]	n.	收敛性
rigorous * ['rigərəs]	a.	严格的,严厉的
filler-wall		填充墙
software ['sɔftwεə]	n.	软件

Notes

①so that …, and so that … 为两个并列的目的状语从句,修饰主句。

②Looked at…,为过去分词短语,用做时间状语;of which…引导定语从句修饰 three-dimensional elements;impossible to…与 is a forbidding task 为两个并列表语。

③句中 which are…引导定语从句,修饰主句中的 traffic loads;intended to…为过去分词短语做目的状语。

④句中 rigid joints to pin-joints…前省略了谓语 are reduced;in deciding…为介词短语做时间状语。

⑤句中 in which…引导非限定性定语从句,修饰 a trial-and-error procedure。

⑥ 句中 ranging from…to… 为现在分词短语做方式状语,修饰全句。

Exercises

Reading Comprehension

I. Choose the most suitable alternative to complete the following sentences.
  1. Structural analysis is _____ due to specified loads.
     A. the course of existing structures
     B. the process of determining the forces and deformations
     C. the procedure of deciding the structure
     D. the progress of designing the forces and deformations
  2. The most important use of structural analysis is _____.
     A. as a device in structural analysis
     B. as an apparatus in reinforced concrete practice
     C. as an instrument in structural design
     D. as an implement in entire systems
  3. The more realistic the analysis, _____ which it inspires.
     A. the confidence will be greater
     B. the stronger will be the confidence
     C. the confidence will be stronger
     D. the greater will be the confidence
  4. Collapse of a structure will usually occur _____ has been exceeded at critical points.
     A. only before the elastic range of the materials
     B. only earlier than the range of the materials
     C. only long after the elastic range of the materials
     D. only ahead of the elastic range of the materials
  5. For the reason, an important part of the analyst's work is _____.
     A. to simplify the actual structure and loading conditions
     B. the simplicity of the actual structure and loading conditions
     C. to make the actual structure and loading conditions briefly
     D. the simplification of structure and conditions

II. From the list below choose the most appropriate headings for each of the paragraphs in the text, then put the paragraph numbers in the brackets.
   A. Simplifying the actual structure and loading conditions to a model   (   )
   B. Structural analysis   (   )
   C. Simplifying the determination of actual loading conditions   (   )

D. The necessity of structural analysis in structural design ( )
E. Mastering the rigorous methods of analysis ( )
F. The importance of the ultimate strength theory ( )
G. Modern matrix-computer methods ( )
H. A concept leading to a configuration ( )
I. Idealization making the solution more suspect ( )

III. Complete the following sentences with the information given in the text.

1. _____, the cost of the structure is estimated, _____ and _____ are revised.
2. _____, an important part of the analyst's work is the simplification of the actual structure and loading conditions _____ to rational analysis.
3. _____ analyst must likewise be versed _____ and its use in digital computers _____ programs or software.
4. In the design of structures, _____ a concept leading to a configuration _____ analyzed.
5. _____ have revolutionized structural analysis _____, thus leading to more reliable predictions _____.

Vocabulary

I. Choose one word or expression which is the most similar in meaning to the word underlined in the given sentence.

1. An elastic theory can determine a safe approximation to the strength of <u>ductile</u> structures.
   A. stretchy   B. extensive   C. widespread   D. lengthy
2. I hope your mother does not <u>contemplate</u> coming to stay with us.
   A. pretend   B. intend   C. attend   D. extend
3. They made a nuclear arms treaty with many <u>provisions</u>.
   A. qualifications   B. regulations   C. specifications   D. conditions
4. They were making a <u>rigorous</u> search for dutiable goods.
   A. tough   B. stern   C. hard   D. rigid
5. The figure we have is only an <u>approximation</u> of the actual cost involved.
   A. match   B. proportion   C. approach   D. equilibrium

II. Match the words in Column A with their corresponding definitions or explanations in Column B.

A	B
1. elastic	a. an arrangement of the mechanical tissue of a stem or leaf in such a way that effective support is given to the member
2. girder	b. normally a reinforced concrete floor supported, at intervals, on beams and columns

3. software   c. having the tendency to go back to the normal or previous size or shape after being pulled or pressed

4. slab   d. a hard main structure round which something is built or made

5. beam   e. general term for programming or compiling accessories used for computing or data-processing systems

         f. long horizontal piece of squared timber, or of steel light alloy, concrete, supported at both ends, used to carry the weight of a building, etc.

         g. something which relates to a force which produces power or movement

         h. a particular stage in a process, or in the gradual development of something such as a society or person's life

Reading Material A

Matrix Analysis of Structures by the Stiffness Method

Structural analysis is concerned with the determination of stresses and displacements in a structure for a given loading so that the designer can provide sufficient resistance to resist the stresses developed. Although the designer has to design many complex structures, most of the structures in practice fall into the following two categories.

(a) Skeletal structures. Skeletal structures are easily identified by the presence of a framework or 'skeleton' built from elements such as bars and beams connected at joints. Typical examples of skeletal structures are two-dimensional (2-D) and three-dimensional (3-D) pin-jointed structures (trusses), 2-D and 3-D rigid-jointed structures (plane and space frames) plane grids, etc. In the great majority of such structures, the members are straight although plane grids in bridge structures very often contain curved members.

(b) Continuum structures. In this type of structure, the material is not concentrated along certain members as in the skeletal structures but the material is continuously distributed with no clearly identifiable members or joints. Typical examples of continuum structures are plates, shells, walls, dams, etc.

Over the years, innumerable methods for analysing structures have been developed. Many of these methods were geared to the manual analysis of specific structures. However, the ready availability of digital computers has revolutionized especially the analysis and to a lesser extent the design of structures. Digital computers can be programmed to perform extremely complex calculations with a minimum input of basic data. Consequently, many methods of structural analysis which exploit the power of the computers have been developed over the last three decades. However, at the present time, the method known as the stiffness (or displacement) method is the one most widely used. One of the very attractive features of the stiffness method is that it enables the development of a unified approach to the analysis of complex skeletal and continuum structures. ①This unity of concept enables a program which can analyse pin-jointed structures to be modified with minimum effort to analyse another type of structure such as, say, rigid-jointed structures. In this chapter the analysis of skeletal structures by the stiffness method will be described in detail. The programming aspects will be discussed in the succeeding chapters.

Structural analysis-Basic Conditions to be Satisfied

Every method of structural analysis has to satisfy the following basic requirements in order that the solution is 'correct'. The conditions are as follows.

(a) Equilibrium between the internal stresses (or, for skeletal structures, stress resultants such as axial forces, bending moments, shear forces, torques, etc.) and external loads must be maintained throughout the structure.

(b) The displacements and their derivatives must satisfy the basic continuity requirements as required by the specific structure. For example, in a pin-jointed structure, all the members meeting at a joint must experience the same displacement in two orthogonal directions.② Similarly, in a 2-D rigid-jointed structure, continuity of displacement requires continuity of both slopes and displacements.

(c) The stresses and strains must satisfy the prescribed material laws.

(d) The stresses and strains must satisfy the prescribed forces and displacements at the boundaries such as supports, etc.

Element in a Structure—The Building Block

In a skeletal structure, the basic building block is the member or the element in a structure. The structure is an assembly of elements connected at joints (also called nodes). It is therefore important to understand the derivation of the 'properties' of the element and the way in which the basic requirements of equilibrium, etc. are satisfied.③ In addition, because the element will be joined to other members only at its ends, attention will be concentrated on deriving the relationship between the forces and the corresponding displacements at the ends of the element. In the following sections, the relationship between the forces and the displacements at the ends of some common elements such as bars, beams and shafts will be derived.

Notes

①刚度法引人注目的特征之一是使复杂的杆系结构和连续体结构能够统一进行分析。
②例如，在铰接结构中，相交于一点的所有构件在两个互相垂直方向上必然产生同样的位移。
③因此了解单元"特征"的推导以及需要满足的平衡条件等方面的基本要求是很重要的。

Reading Material B

Equilibrium of Single Members

Before looking further into the subject of static equilibrium, the concept of the rigid body should be introduced. In statics, it becomes convenient, if not necessary, to ignore the small deformations and displacements which take place when a member is loaded. To do this, we pretend that the materials used for all structural elements and supports are rigid, having the property of infinite stiffness. ① We assume that members do not stretch, compress, or bend in any way and that their geometry, therefore, remains constant. This is, of course, never true. Even though structural materials are very stiff, they all deform slightly even under small loads. However, the assumption that structural bodies are rigid greatly simplifies many situations in terms of static equilibrium and, in most cases, introduces an insignificant amount of error. An example of the type of minute change, which is generally ignored, is the shortening of span that takes place when a beam deflects into an arc. ② Depending upon the type of loading, minor changes in the upward reactions at the supports would also occur. Not only would such changes be insignificant if expressed in percentage terms, but would also be difficult to consider quantitatively because, like other deformations, they vary with the load. ③

Once all of the external forces have been resolved in terms of statics, the stresses and strains within the various elements of the structure are examined. At this point, it is critical that material deformations are not ignored. The rigid-body concept is useful only for the determination of external forces. (It is generally valid but can require modification when applied to the statics of more complicated structural problems.)

While the idea of a structure that is rigid for some analytical operations but not for others may seem incongruous to the novice, a little experience will quickly provide the rationale and judgment behind this concept. ④

In structural analysis, the principles of statics are used to determine reactive forces, which are responses to the applied loads. These reactions always develop the appropriate magnitudes and directions, such that the end result is one of equilibrium. In other words, under the combined action of the loads and reactions, each element of the structure has zero tendency to translate and zero tendency to rotate.

Determining the needed reactive forces is made easier if the analyst makes a sketch of the structure or element, showing all the forces involved (known and unknown). Such a sketch is called a free-body diagram (FBD), and most structural designers consider making such a diagram the first step in any statics problem. A free-body diagram shows the body in isolation or cut "free" from everything adjacent to it. The effects of all such removed objects are shown as forces acting at the appropriate locations. We have already used these diagrams in this chapter without calling them by name.

Notes

①为此我们假定用于全部结构构件的材料以及各支承都是刚性的，均具有无限大的刚度。

②微小改变类型的一个例子是当一个梁弯曲成弧形时其跨度变小。这种微小改变通常是被忽略的。

③如果用百分比来表示，这种变化不仅无关紧要而且像其他变形一样，由于随荷载大小而改变，所以很难进行定量地考虑。

④我们在某些分析过程中，将结构看成刚性的而在其它情况下看成非刚性的。这种概念对初学者来说，似乎两者不太一致。只需有一点经验就可防止这种概念的形成和判断有误。

UNIT SEVEN

Text Properties of Concrete and Reinforced Concrete

[1] Concrete is a man-made conglomerate stone composed of essentially four ingredients: portland cement, water, sand, and coarse aggregate. The cement and water combine to make a paste that binds the sand and stones together. Ideally, the aggregates are graded so that the volume of paste is at a minimum, merely surrounding every piece with a thin layer.① Most structural concrete Is stone concrete, but structural lightweight concrete (roughly two-thirds the density of stone concrete) is becoming increasingly popular.

[2] Concrete is essentially a compressive material having almost no tensile strength, so concrete's weakness in tension also causes it to be weak in shear. These deficiencies are overcome by using steel bars for reinforcement at the places where tensile and shearing stresses are generated.② Under load, reinforced concrete beams actually have numerous minute cracks which run at right angles to the direction of major tensile stresses. The tensile forces at such locations are being taken completely by the steel "re-bars."

[3] The compressive strength of a given concrete is a function of the quality and proportions of its constituents and the manner in which the fresh concrete is cured. (Curing is the process of hardening during which time the concrete must be prevented from "drying out", as the presence of water is necessary for the chemical action to progress.) Coarse aggregate that is hard and well graded is particularly essential for quality concrete. The most important factor governing the strength, however, is the percentage of water used in the mix. A minimum amount of water is needed for proper hydration of the cement. Additional water is needed for handling and placing the concrete, but excess amounts cause the strength to drop markedly.

[4] These and other topics are fully covered in the booklet, "Design and Control of Concrete Mixtures," published by the Portland Cement Association. This is an excellent reference, treating both concrete mix design and proper construction practices. The American Concrete Institute publishes a widely adopted code specifying the structural requirements for reinforced concrete.

[5] Concrete is known as the "formable" or "moldable" structural material. Compared to other materials, it is easy to make curvilinear members and surfaces with concrete. It has no inherent texture but adopts the texture of the forming material, so it can range widely in surface appearance. It is relatively inexpensive to make, both in terms of raw materials and labor, and the basic ingredients of portland cement are available the world over. (It should be noted, however, that the necessary reinforcing bars for concrete may not be readily available in less-developed countries.)

[6] The best structural use of reinforced concrete, in terms of the characteristics of the material, is in those structures requiring continuity and or rigidity. It has a monolithic quality

which automatically makes fixed or continuous connections. These moment-resistant joints are such that many low-rise concrete buildings do not require a secondary bracing system for lateral loads. In essence, a concrete beam joins a concrete column very differently from the way steel and wood pieces join, and the sensitive designer will not ignore this difference. (These remarks do not apply to precast structural elements, which are usually not joined in a continuous manner.)

[7] Concrete is naturally fireproof and needs no separate protection system. Because of its mass, it can also serve as an effective barrier to sound transmission.

[8] In viewing the negative aspects, concrete is unfortunately quite heavy and it is often noted that a concrete structure expends a large portion of its capacity merely carrying itself.③ Attempts to make concrete less dense, while maintaining high quality levels, have generally resulted in increased costs.④ Nevertheless, use of lightweight concrete can sometimes result in overall economies.

[9] Concrete requires more quality control than most other building materials. Modern transit-mixed concrete suppliers are available to all U.S. urban areas and the mix is usually of a uniformly high quality. Field-or-job-mixed concrete requires knowledgeable supervision, however. In any type of concrete work, missing or mislocated reinforcing bars can result in elements with reduced load capacities. Poor handling and/or curing conditions can seriously weaken any concrete. For these and other reasons, most building codes require independent field inspections at various stages of construction.

[10] Proper concrete placement is also somewhat dependent upon the ambient weather conditions. Extremely high temperatures and, more important, those below (or near) freezing can make concrete work very difficult.

New Words and Expressions

conglomerate [kən'glɔmərit]	n.	砾岩, 石材
ingredient * [in'gri:diənt]	n.	成分
aggregate * ['ægrigeit]	n.	骨料
deficiency * [di'fiʃənsi]	n.	缺乏
re-bar = reinforcing bar	n.	钢筋
constituent * [kən'stitjuənt]	n.	成分, 要素
hydration [hai'dreiʃən]	n.	水化(作用)
excess [ik'ses]	a.	超量的
booklet ['buklit]	n.	小册子
moldable = mouldable	a.	可塑的
curvilinear ['kə:vi'liniə]	a.	曲线的
markedly ['mɑ:kidli]	ad.	显著地

texture * ['tekstʃə]	n.	纹理,质地
rigidity * [ri'dʒiditi]	n.	刚性,刚度
brace * [breis]	n.,v.	支柱;撑牢
in essence		大体上,本质上
monolithic * [ˌmɔnəu'liθik]	a.	整体的
precast ['priː'kɑːst]	vt.	预制
supervision [ˌsjuːpə'viʒən]	n.	监督
ambient * ['æmbiənt]	a.	周围的
transit-mixed *	a.	混合运输的
field-or-job-mixed	a.	现场或临时的
moment-resistant	n.	抗扭矩
placement ['pleismənt]	n.	灌(浇)筑
mislocated [ˌmisləu'keitid]	a.	放错位置的
inspection [in'spekʃən]	n.	检查

Notes

①surrounding 为现在分词短语,做主句的方式状语。

②by using steel bar…中的介词 by 引导的短语相当于 by means of,在句中做方式状语；where 引导的定语从句修饰 the places。

③In viewing…意为:考虑到；carrying itself 是分词短语做伴随状语,修饰全句。

④由连词 while（而）连接的不定式短语 to make concrete…和现在分词短语 maintaining high…,共同做主语 attemps 的后置定语。

Exercises

Reading Comprehension

I. Choose the most suitable alternative to complete the following sentences.

1. Concrete consists of especially four ingredient:_____.
   A. water, cement, stone chips and sand
   B. portland cement, coarse aggregate, water and stone
   C. rough aggregate, portland cement, water and sand
   D. coarse aggregate, sand, water and clay

2. These deficiencies are overcome _____.
   A. by using iron band for reinforcement only
   B. by using steel bars for reinforcement
   C. by using load stone for reinforcement to a great extent

D. by using aluminium plate for reinforcement
3. Compared to other materials, concrete _____.
   A. has inherent texture
   B. is inexpensive in less-developed countries
   C. is available all over the world
   D. can be used to make curvilinear members and surfaces easily
4. Concrete demands _____.
   A. more quantity control than other materials
   B. less quality control than other building materials
   C. more quality control than other building materials
   D. less quantity control than other materials
5. Attemps to make concrete less dense, _____ have generally resulted in increased costs.
   A. while keeping high quality levels
   B. when being maintained high quality levels
   C. while having been kept high quality levels
   D. as they are maintained high quality levels

II. From the list below choose the most appropriate headings for each of the paragraphs in the text, than put the paragraph numbers in the brackets.
   A. The monolithic quality of reinforced concrete   (   )
   B. Poor handling and curing conditions weaking the concrete   (   )
   C. A man-made conglomerate stone   (   )
   D. "Formable" or "moldable" structural material   (   )
   E. A compressive material having almost no tensile strength   (   )
   F. Concrete placement depending on the weather conditions   (   )
   G. The percentage of water in the mix   (   )
   H. The natural fireproof of concrete   (   )
   I. Code specifying the structural requirements for reinforced concrete (   )
   J. Overall economies by using lightweight concrete   (   )

III. Complete the following sentences with the information given in the text.
   1. Additional water is needed _____, but excess amounts cause the strength _____.
   2. Concrete is known as the "_____" or "_____" structural material.
   3. _____ publishes a widely adopted code specifying the structural requirements for _____.
   4. _____ are available to all U. S. urban areas and mix is usually of a _____.
   5. Because of its mass, _____ to sound transmission.

Vocabulary

I. Choose one word or expression which is the most similar in meaning to the word underlined in the given sentence.

1. Rickets can result from a diet deficiency in Vitamin D.
   A. inefficiency   B. inadequacy   C. infrequency   D. intimacy
2. Don't think that Europe is monolithic and all countries in Europe must make the same decision.
   A. vast   B. entire   C. thorough   D. composite
3. This process is called photosynthesis and one of the ingredients it requires is hydrogen.
   A. components   B. factors   C. duplicates   D. configurations
4. All of these primitive sea creatures had well developed lateral fins.
   A. angle   B. front   C. side   D. ambient
5. The greater the tensile strength of a wire, the greater the weight it will support without breaking.
   A. expansive   B. energetic   C. excess   D. oversize

II. Match the words in Column A with their corresponding definitions or explanations in Column B.

A	B
1. deficiency	a. the mode of union or disposition, in regard to each other, of the elementary constituent parts in the structure of any body or material
2. code	b. amount by which something is short of what is correct or needed
3. cement	c. a mixture of cement, sand, and gravel, with water in varying proportions according to the use which is to be made of it
4. texture	d. collection of laws arranged in a system
5. concrete	e. a material for uniting other materials or articles
	f. the degree of hotness or coldness measured with respect to an arbitrary zero
	g. a material such as pieces of rock added to cement to make concrete
	h. the quality of stiffness that sth has when it is rigid

Reading Material A

Property of Structural Steel

Steel is the strongest and stiffest building material in common use today. Relative to wood and concrete, it is a high-technology material made by highly refined and controlled processes. Structural steel has a uniformly high strength in tension and compression and is also very good in shear. It comes in a range of yield strengths made by adjusting the chemistry of the material in its molten state. It is the most consistent of all structural materials and is, for all practical purposes, homogeneous and isotropic, meaning it has like characteristics in all directions.① (By contrast, wood is anisotropic.)

The greatest asset to steel is its strength and plastic reserve. It is highly ductile and deforms greatly before failing if overloaded. Because of steel's strength, the individual members of a frame are usually small in cross section and have very little visual mass.

Steel is a linear material and can be economically made into a visual curve only by using a segmented geometry. It is most appropriately used in rectilinear structures where bolted or welded connections are easy to make. The structural shapes (i. e., pipes, tubes, channels, angles, and wide-flange sections) are manufactured to uniform dimensions having low tolerances. They are fully prepared (cut, trimmed or milled, drilled or punched, etc.) in a fabrication shop, remote from the site, and then delivered ready for erection. Such structures go up rapidly with a minimum of on-site labor. The most popular form of construction used today is referred to as shop-welded, field-bolted. In this method the various clip angles, beam seats, and so on, are welded to the members in a shop and then the members are bolted together in the field.

A major disadvantage to structural steel is its need to be fire-protected in most applications. It loses its strength at around 500 °C and will then yield rapidly under low loads. A few municipalities require that all structural steel be fire-protected, and most codes will not permit any exposed elements to be within approximately 4m of a combustible fire source.

The making of steel requires large physical plants and a high capital outlay, and therefore relatively few countries of the world have extensive mill facilities. The cost of manufacturing, coupled with the cost of transportation, can make steel a relatively expensive material.② Just the same, in most urban areas, concrete and steel are quite competitive with one another in terms of inplace construction costs.

Continuity in the connections is much harder to achieve in steel than in concrete, and most buildings are constructed with simple connections or ones that are only partially moment-resistent. Some type of lateral load bracing system is almost always required in a steel-framed building and must be considered early in the design process.

Rolled steel is manufactured in a wide range of strengths. The standard low-carbon, mild steel in use today has a yield strength of 250 MPa. Steel plate can be obtained with an F_y value of almost 700 MPa, and most standard shapes can be rolled in steel as strong as 450 MPa, although this can be expensive. Examples and problems in this text are limited to shapes of F_y, $=250$ MPa and $F_y=345$ MPa. These particular values are the most common ones, with the lower 250-MPa strength being the most frequently specified. ③

Information about the various kinds of steel available can be obtained directly from manufacturers and fabricators. The reader is also advised to purchase the latest edition of the Manual of Steel Construction, published by the American Institute of Steel Construction. It is an indispensable reference work for the design professional.

Notes

①钢材是所有结构材料中最具一致性的一种,并且对各种实用情况都具有沿方向存在同一特性的均匀性和各向同性的性质。
②制造成本再加运输成本,使钢材成为一种比较昂贵的材料。
③这些特定的值是最常用的,而且往往规定其中的较低强度250MPa。

Reading Material B

Nature of Wood and Masonry

Wood is a natural material and has a broad range of physical properties because of the different characteristics of its many species. Softwoods such as fir, pine, and hemlock are most often used for structural applications because they are more plentiful (grow fast and tall) and are easier to fabricate. These woods are generally strong in tension and compression in a direction parallel to the grain and weak when stressed perpendicularly to the grain. ① Wood is also weak in shear because of its tendency to split along the natural grain laminations.

Wood is light and soft compared to most other structural materials and is easily shaped and fastened together. A minimum of materials-handling equipment is needed to erect wood structures because of their weight. It is also very versatile in terms of its adaptability to the making of geometric shapes and even nonlinear forms.

Most softwoods are fairly ductile and will not fail suddenly when overloaded. Because of their lack of homogeneity or uniformity, the allowable stresses are quite low compared to failure stresses. Consequently, when wood structures are properly engineered, a statistically high margin of safety is present. Wood is often known as the "forgiving" material because of its apparent ability to sustain loads not accounted for when the structure was designed. ②

Wood, on the other hand, is not very stiff. It is subject to excessive deflection and creep deformation if not designed with these characteristics in mind. It is prone to damage by fire and to deterioration by moisture and insects. It expands and contracts with variations in humidity, markedly so in the direction perpendicular to the grain. Timber structures that are to be exposed to the elements must be carefully treated or highly maintained to preserve their integrity.

The American Institute of Timber Construction publishes the Manual of Timber Construction③ and the reader is referred to it for more extensive information on the properties and use of wood. The National Forest Products Association publishes some excellent design aids and data books for use by the structural designer.

Like concrete, brick and concrete masonry units are strong in compression and weak in tension. These materials have traditionally been used in walls, both bearing and nonbearing. Usually, wall thicknesses required by code specifications to prevent lateral instability are such that the actual compressive stresses are low. Crushing is seldom an important design constraint. ④

Masonry walls are more permanent than wood walls and provide effective barriers to both fire and noise. They are less expensive and often more attractive than formed concrete walls. Brick generally has more variation of pattern and texture than does concrete block, but is also more expensive.

It is becoming increasingly common to use reinforced concrete block for retaining walls and structural pilasters. In this construction, individual reinforcing bars are grouted in some of the vertically aligned cells of the concrete units and serve as tensile reinforcement. This greatly increases the lateral load capacity of the block. Reinforcing can also be placed in special channel-shaped blocks to serve as lintels and tie beams. Brick can be reinforced by using two wythes to create a cavity for grout and reinforcing bars. ⑤ The brick not only serves as formwork but also carries compressive forces under load.

Notes

①一般来讲，这些木材沿平行于纤维方向拉压时强度高，而沿垂直纤维方向拉压时强度低。
②木材被认为是"低档次"的材料，因为在设计结构时没有考虑它表面上的承载能力。
③"美国木结构施工学会"；
　《木结构施工手册》。
④压碎的情况在设计中很少成为约束条件。
⑤可采用Y形槽以提供胶泥和加筋杆的空间来对砖砌体配筋。

UNIT EIGHT

Text   Building Code (Ⅰ)

[1]   A building code is a statute, in the form of detailed regulations, that has been enacted by a municipality or other government entity to ensure that all the buildings constructed within its jurisdiction meet certain minimum standards of health and safety. ① The building code has its legal justification in the inherent power of any government to protect its citizens from any harm likely to come to them because of unhealthy or unsafe conditions.

[2]   Building codes, therefore, are concerned with such things as structural adequacy, the quality and strength of the materials used, sound workmanship, the correct installation of approved electrical wiring and equipment, the correct installation of approved gas-, coal-, or oil-heating equipment and their piping, the correct installation of approved sanitary plumbing fixtures and their piping, the fire resistance of the materials used, and the existence of fire exits.

[3]   In most municipalities, the plans for all new construction must be approved by officials of the buildings department before construction begins, and these same officials must have access to the property at all times and be able to inspect all equipment, materials, and workmanship before the building is approved for occupancy. If the equipment, workmanship, or materials do not meet the standards of the building code, these officials have the authority to order that the necessary changes be made before they issue a certificate of occupancy, as it is called.

[4]   Once a building has been approved and occupied, if the owner should thereafter want to make a basic alteration in the electrical, heating, or plumbing systems, or a basic change in the structure, the buildings department must approve the alterations beforehand and inspect the workmanship and materials after the alteration has been completed. If the job is signed off by a licensed electrician or plumber, adequacy of workmanship and materials is usually assumed, although the buildings department always reserves the right to make a subsequent inspection and order any changes it thinks necessary.

[5]   The impulse that led to the development of building codes was humanitarian. Without the legal restraint imposed by a code, nothing prevented a builder from putting up the cheapest, shoddiest, and most densely packed dwellings he could get away with. Perhaps the best-known examples of such jerry-built construction in the United States were the cold-water tenements —— the "old law" tenements —— that once covered most of the Lower East Side of Manhattan, and much of the other sections of New York City as well②. The crowded, unsanitary conditions that existed in these tenements, and the large number of fires that occurred because of these conditions, led to the development and adoption of building codes.

[6]   The codes that have been adopted by most large- and medium-size cities in the United States are a mixture of engineering knowledge, local building customs, and an accommodation to local political realities. Originally, building codes were of the specifications type, which re-

quired that all construction be accomplished using specified materials in a specified way. ③ The builder has very little leeway in the materials he can select or the methods of construction he can use. One curious example of how this specification-type building code has influenced building styles was the requirement in New York City that the rooftop water-storage tanks that are connected to standby fire-sprinkler systems be constructed of wood staves. As a result, anyone who has ever looked down on midtown Manhattan from a skyscraper has been struck by the sight of innumerable wooden water tanks with conical roofs perched rather incongruously on top of all that steel and concrete.

[7]　　Specification-type building codes were probably a necessity in a day when speculative builders tried to get by using the cheapest materials they could buy, assembled in the most slipshod manner.④ But times changed, and new materials were developed. Since World War II there has been a swing toward building codes of the performance type, in which the performance standards of a material or structure are outlined and the builder is free to select whatever materials or building techniques will meet these standards.

[8]　　For example, a specification-type code for a house sewer will simply specify that cast-iron pipe of a certain quality and size be used and that the pipe be installed in a specified manner. The plumbing contractor has no choice or say in the manner. In a performance-type building code, however, the code will specify that the piping not be affected by any corrosive or harmful substances in the sewage or in the soil in which the pipe is buried, that the pipe meet certain minimum strength requirements, and that the pipe not be affected by temperature changes within a specified range.⑤ The plumbing contractor is free to use plastic pipe, cast-iron pipe, or gold pipe if he wants to, as long as he can show the local buildings officials that the pipe does in fact meet their standards.

New Words and Expressions

statute['stætjuːt]	n.	法规
enact[i'nækt]	v.	制定
adequacy * ['ædikwəsi]	n.	适当
municipality[mju(ː)ˌnisi'pæliti]	n.	市,市政
entity['entiti]	n.	实体,统一体
jurisdiction * [ˌdʒuəris'dikʃən]	n.	管辖权,权限
sanitary['sænitəri]	a.	卫生的
fixture * ['fikstʃə]	n.	(pl. 房屋的)固定装置
impulse['impʌls]	n.	冲动,推动
thereafter[ðɛər'ɑːftə]	ad.	由此,以后
sign off		停止活动
humanitarian[hju(ː)ˌmæni'tɛəriən]	a.	人道主义的

impose[im'pəuz]	vt.	把…强加给
shoddy['ʃɔdi]	a.	质量差的
dwelling['dweliŋ]	n.	住所，寓所
tenement['tenimənt]	n.	住屋，一套房间
standhy[s'tændbai]	a.	备用的，辅助的
sprinkler['spriŋklə]	n.	洒，喷淋
leeway['li:wei]	n.	可允许的误差
jerry['dʒeri]	a.	偷工减料的
conical['kɔnikəl]	a.	圆锥形的
perch[pə:tʃ]	vt.	放置…于高处
stave[steiv]	n.	桶板
incongruously[in'kɔŋgruəsli]	ad.	不调和地，不一致地
speculative['spekjulətiv]	a.	投机的
slipshod['slipʃɔd]	a.	马虎的，潦草的
contractor[kən'træktə]	n.	承包人
corrosive[kə'rəusiv]	a.	腐蚀性的
sewage['sjuəridʒ]	n.	污水
plumb[plʌm]	n.	管子，铅管

Notes

①句中第一个 that 引出定语从句，修饰 statute；第二个 that 引出宾语从句，做 ensure 的宾语；in the form of detailed regulations 用做插入语。

②cold-water tenements "冷水公寓"，指那些没有热水供应的廉租公寓。

③which 引出非限定性定语从句；using…是分词短语做伴随状语。

④句中 by using 做方式状语；assembled 与 tried 是并列谓语。

⑤specify 后有三个 that 引导的宾语从句，句中省略了 should。

Exercises

Reading Comprehension

Ⅰ. Choose the most suitable alternative to complete the following sentences.

1. A building code is _____.

   A. a form of detailed regulations

   B. the minimum standards of health and safety

   C. a government jurisdiction

   D. a law that is made to ensure that all the buildings are strong and safe to live in.

2. When a building is under construction the officials of the building department must be allowed to enter the building _____.
   A. to visit the building site regularly
   B. to work with the workers and check the building materials
   C. to determine whether the equipment materials and workmanship is up to the standards of building codes
   D. to find out whether there are enough manpowers for the building
3. Building codes of the specification-type required that _____.
   A. the builder use specified materials in a specified way
   B. the builder select materials, building techniques freely
   C. the builder be free to select materials and the methods of construction
   D. the builder use specified materials in a required way
4. Since World War II the codes have developed into the performance type in which _____.
   A. the builders can do whatever they like
   B. the builders have more choices in material structures and building techniques
   C. the materials and building techniques are specified
   D. the builders have little choice in materials or the methods of construction
5. The plumbing contractor _____ as long as he can show the local building official that the pipe does in fact meet their standards.
   A. is required to choose plastic pipe only
   B. is free to use both cast-iron and plastic pipe
   C. is forced to use gold pipe
   D. has right to use whatever pipe he may get

II. From the list below choose the most appropriate headings for each of the paragraphs in the text, then put the paragraph numbers in the brackets.
   A. The difference between the specification type and performance type   (   )
   B. The reason for the development of the building codes   (   )
   C. The necessity to get the approval before making a basic alternative   (   )
   D. The purpose of using the building codes   (   )
   E. The right of the officials of the building department   (   )
   F. The use of the performance type due to the development of new materials (   )
   G. The facts concerning the building codes   (   )
   H. The requirement of the specification type   (   )

III. Complete the following sentences with the information given in the text.
   1. Building codes _____ with such things.
   2. If the equipment, workmanship or materials do not _____ of the building code, these officials _____ that the necessary changes he made.
   3. Originally, building codes were of the specification type, which required that _____

using _____ in a _____.
4. Since World War II there has been a swing toward building codes of the performance type, in which _____ of a material or structure _____ and the builder is _____ whatever materials or _____ will meet these standards.
5. The plumbing contractor is free to use _____, _____ or _____ if he wants to, _____ he can show that the pipe does in fact meet their standards.

Vocabulary

I. Choose one word or expression which is the most similar in meaning to the word underlined in the given sentence.
1. The sanitary authorities of the town inspect the sanitary arrangement in every house.
   A. healthful   B. salutary   C. sound   D. hale
2. In his unhappiness he had come even to question his entity.
   A. existence   B. capability   C. wit   D. tyranny
3. He gave the first strong impulse to a study of this subject in Canada.
   A. appetite   B. lure   C. motive   D. objective
4. The cabinet was put together in a hurried, slipshod way.
   A. stale   B. sloppy   C. unfresh   D. unclean
5. This dilapidated old house was incongruous with the skyscrapers.
   A. disagreeable   B. inseparate   C. insane   D. inconsistent

II. Match the words in Column A with their corresponding definition or explanations in Column B.

A	B
1. statute	a. a law passed by Parliament or other law-making body
2. jurisdiction	b. town district, city with local self-government
3. tenement	c. administration of justice; legal authority
4. sewer	d. under-ground channel to carry off sewage and rain water to centre for treatment
5. municipality	e. any dwelling-house; any kind of permanent property
	f. strongly made building used for defence at some important place
	g. binding agreement; agreement to supply goods, do work, etc at a fixed price
	h. not providing good support

Reading Material A

Building Code (Ⅱ)

The spread of performance-type codes has been helped enormously by the materials specifications published by the American National Standards Institute,[①] (ANSI; formerly the American Standards Association), by the American Society for Testing and Materials (ASTM), by branches of the U.S. government, especially the Department of Commerce, and by an enormous number of specialized industry groups. To ensure the adequacy of any material used for construction, all a local building code need do is specify, in the case of house sewers, for example, that the polyvinyl chloride pipe used. (if a plastic pipe is being used) meets standard specification D 2665—73 published by the ASTM.

Small municipalities are not in a position to undertake independent studies of building materials and construction techniques and then publish their own building codes based on their findings. They have come instead to depend on the work being done by four nonprofit organizations whose membership consists of building officials. Those organizations have published model codes that all municipalities are free to adopt in whole or in part. The virtues of adopting a model code are that the municipality is assured of obtaining a well-thoughtout and up-to-date performance-type building code based on sound construction practices, a code that is updated periodically in the light of changing conditions and the availability of new materials.[②] All the model-code organizations are prepared to help a municipality establish a buildings department complete with all the necessary forms and procedures.

The four organizations and their published codes are as follows:

American Insurance Association (formerly the National Board of Fire Underwriters)-National Building Code.

Building Officials and Code Administrators International(formerly Building Officials and Conference of America)-Basic Building Code

International Conference of Building Officials(formerly the Pacific Coast Building Officials Conference)-Uniform Building Code.

Southern Building Code Congress-Standard Building Code.

These codes are not intended primarily for one-and two-family dwellings, although they do apply to dwellings also. In 1971 these four organizations joined together to publish a model building code that is devoted exclusively to dwellings. The One and Two Family Dwelling Code, which is essentially a distillation of all four codes as they apply to dwellings.

There are several other model codes that are of importance to builders of one- and two-family dwellings. The National Fire Protection Association publishes an enormous range of books and pamphlets dealing with the construction of fire-resistant buildings, the use of fire-resistant materials, and fire-fighting procedures and equipment. Among their publications is the National Electrical Code, which most municipalities have adopted in toto as a basic part of their own buildings codes. The National Electrical Code contains approved methods of installing electrical wiring and equipment for all types of buildings. Licensed electricians are required by most municipalities to be thoroughly familiar with this code; the electricians must pass a test based on their knowledge of the code before they can receive their licenses. ③

In 1972 the National Fire Protection Association published an abridgement of the electrical code called the Electrical Code for One-and Two-family Dwellings. Anyone wiring or rewiring a house should install the wiring according to the requirements of this publication.

Three of the model organizations mentioned above have also promulgated model plumbing codes, which are as follows:
BOCA-Basic Plumbing Code
ICBO-Uniform Plumbing Code
SBCC-Standard Plumbing Code
These codes were published because their predecessor, the National Plumbing Code, which had been published last in 1944 as a cooperative effort of the United States government and many engineering societies and industry associations, had fallen hopelessly out of date. ④ As with the electrical code, most municipalities have now adopted one of the above model plumbing codes in full as a basic part of their own building code.

Notes

①美国标准学会颁布的材料规范极大地促进了性能型法规的推广和应用。
②采用一种样式的法规优点是市政当局确实得到了建立在实践经验基础上最新的性能型建筑规范。这种规范是按照情况的变化和新材料的应用定期地进行修订。
③大部分市政管理部门要求所有持有合格证的电工都完全熟悉这个法规。
④因为前国家管道规范是在1944年为协助美国政府和许多工程协会以及工业协会而颁布的，早已过时，因此颁步了现有的规范。

Reading Material B

Building Code (Ⅲ)

A building code is a set of detailed regulations to ensure that all the buildings meet certain minimum standards of health and safety. Building codes have been enacted to protect citizens from any harm likely to come to them because of unhealthy or unsafe conditions. ①

The plan for all new construction must be approved by officials of the buildings department before construction begins. These same officials must have the right of entering the property at all times. They must be able to inspect all equipment, materials, and workmanship before the building is approved for occupancy. If the equipment, workmanship, or materials do not meet the standards of the building code, these officials have the right to order that the necessary changes be made.

Occasionally, the owner of a building might want to make a basic alteration in the electrical, heating, or plumbing systems. He may also want to make a basic change in the structure. In this case, the buildings department must approve the alterations beforehand. After the alterations has been completed, the officials must once again inspect the workmanship and materials.

Originally, building codes were of the specifications type. They required that all construction be accomplished using specified materials in a specified way. The builder has very little choice in the materials or the methods of construction. Here is a curious example of how this specification-type building code has influenced building styles in New York City. The requirement was that the rooftop water-storage tanks be constructed of wood staves. As a result, anyone who has ever looked down on midtown Manhattan from a skyscraper has been struck by the sight of innumerable wooden water tanks with conical roofs standing high on top of all that steel and concrete.②

Specification-type building codes were probably a necessity at that time. Builders tried to get by using the cheapest materials they could buy. They also assembled in the most careless manner. But times changed, and new materials were developed. Since World War Ⅱ there has been a significant change toward building codes of the performance type. In this type of code the performance standards of a material or structure are outlined. The builder is free to select materials or building techniques which will meet these standards.

For example, a specification-type code for a house sewer will simply specify that cast iron pipe of a certain quality and size be used. It will also specify that the pipe be installed in a specified manner. The plumbing contractor has no choice or say in the matter.③ In a performance-type building code, however, the code will specify that the piping not be affected by any corrosive or harmful substances in the sewage or in the soil in which the pipe is buried. The code will also require that the pipe meet certain minimum strength requirements. In addition, the code will specify that the pipe not be affected by temperature changes within a specified range. The plumbing contractor is free to use plastic pipe, cast-iron pipe, or gold pipe if he wants to, as long as he can show that the pipe does in fact meet the specified standards.

Notes

①建筑规范是为了使公民免受不健康或不安全条件而颁布的。
②结果，任何一个从曼哈顿区中部的摩天大楼上往下观看的人都会为所看到的景象大吃一惊；在那全是钢筋和混凝土的顶部，极不协调地耸立着无数圆锥形屋顶的木制水箱。
③管道承包商在这方面没有选择和决定的权力。

UNIT NINE

Text Early History of Cement and Concrete

[1]   Shelter, from the very beginning of man' existence, has demanded the application of the best available technology of the contemporary era. In the earliest ages, structures consisted of rammed earth, or stone blocks laid one on another without benefit of any bonding or cementing medium. Stability of the stone structures depended on the regular setting of the heavy stones. The earliest masonry probably consisted of sun-dried clay bricks, set in regular courses in thin layers of moist mud. When the moist mud dried, a solid clay wall resulted. Construction of this kind was common in the dry desert areas of the world.

[2]   Burnt gypsum as a cementing material was developed early in the Egyptian period and was apparently used in construction of some of the pyramids. Later the Greeks and Romans discovered methods of burning limestone to produce quicklime which was subsequently slaked for use in making mortar. Both the Greeks and the Romans learned that certain fine soil or earth, when mixed with the lime and the sand, produced a superior cementing material. The Greek material, a volcanic tuff from the island of Santorin, is still used in that part of the world. The best of the materials used by the Romans was a tuff or ash from the vicinity of Pozzuoli near Mt. Vesuvius, hence the name "pozzolan" used to identify a certain type of mineral admixture used in concrete today.

[3]   The cement produced by the Romans was a hydraulic cement, that is, it had the capability of hardening under water. Many of the Roman structures were constructed of a form of concrete, using these materials, and stone masonry was bonded with a mortar similarly composed.[1]

[4]   During the Middle Ages of history, the art of making good mortar was nearly lost, the low point having been reached in about the 11th century, when much inferior material was used. Quality of the lime started to improve at this time and in the 14th century or later the use of pozzolans was again practised.

[5]   One of the most famous projects of the comparatively recent period was the construction of the new Eddystone Lighthouse off the coast of England in 1757—59.[2] John Smeaton, the engineer and designer of the structure, investigated many materials and methods of bonding the stones for the building.

[6]   Engineering and scientific development was beginning to move rapidly at this time, and many researchers in several countries were investigating cementing agents made from gypsum, limestone and other natural materials. One discovery was a method of making a cement by burning a naturally occurring mixture of lime and clay. properties of the natural cement were very erratic because of variations in the proportions in the natural material, although use of this natural cement continued for many years.

[7] In 1824 Joseph Aspdin, a brickmason of Leeds, England, took out a patent on a material he called Portland cement, so called because concrete made with it was supposed to resemble the limestone quarried near Portland, England. Aspdin is generally credited with inventing a method of proportioning limestone and clay, burning the mixture at high temperature to produce clinkers, then grinding the clinkers to produce a hydraulic cement.③ His small kiln, producing about 16 tons of clinker at a time, required several days for each burn. Expansion and development of cement manufacturing was slow for a number of years. About 1850, however, the industry had become well established not only in England, but also in Germany and Belgium.

[8] Shipments to the United States were started in 1868 and reached a peak about 1895, at which time production was well under way in the United States.

[9] Meanwhile the United States production of natural cement had been started early in the 19th century as a result of the demand for cement for construction of the Erie Canal and related works. Subsequent development of the rotary kiln led to large scale production of cement throughout the world.

[10] The use of concrete was expanded by the construction of railroads, bridges, buildings and street pavements. Research in reinforcing concrete with steel rods had been started in France, and the year 1875 saw first use of reinforced concrete in the United States. Much of the concrete at this time contained barely enough water to enable the concrete to be rammed into place by the application of much hand labor. There then ensued a period of wet concrete in which the concrete was flowed into place. Many users of concrete, however, realized the folly of wet mixes, and about 1920 Duff Abrams revealed the results of his research and observations. He stated that the quality of concrete was directly affected by the amount of water in relation to the amount of cement; within reasonable limits, the quality of the concrete decreases as the water-cement ratio goes up. This has become one of the basic laws of concrete technology.

New Words and Expressions

ram [ræm]	vt.	夯实
masonry ['meisnri]	n.	砖石建筑
gypsum ['dʒipsəm]	n.	石膏
pyramid ['pirəmid]	n.	金字塔
limestone ['laimstəun]	n.	石灰石
quicklime = lime	n.	生石灰
slake [sleik]	vt.	（使石灰）熟化
mortar ['mɔːtə]	n.	灰泥，灰浆
vicinity * [vi'siniti]	n.	地区、近处
tuff * [tʌf]	n.	凝灰岩

admixture * [əd'mikstʃə]	n.	添加剂,掺和剂
pozzolan [,pɒtsə'lɑːn]	n.	一种混合水泥(波特兰水泥与火山灰的混合物)
hydraulic [hai'drɔːlik]	a.	水硬的,水力的
hydraulic cement	n.	水硬水泥,水凝水泥
capability * [,keipə'biliti]	n.	性质,能力
erratic [i'rætik]	a.	不稳的,多变的
brickmason ['brikmeisn]	n.	泥瓦匠
quarry ['kwɔri]	vt.	采石,采砂
Leeds [liːdz]	n.	利兹(英格兰地区工业城市)
clinker ['kliŋkə]	n.	(水泥)熟料,渣块、炉渣、
kiln [kiln]	n.	窑
Belgium ['beldʒəm]	n.	比利时(欧洲国家)
shipment ['ʃipmənt]	n.	装运、装载
Erie Canal	n.	伊利运河(美国)
rotary ['rəutəri]	a.	旋转的
pavement ['peivmənt]	n.	铺筑过的路面
ensue [in'sjuː]	vi.	接着发生,接着而来
folly ['fɔli]	n.	蠢事
patent * ['peitənt]	n.	专利证、专利权

Notes

① 现在分词短语 using these materials 做状语,修饰 were constructed；过去分词 composed 做后置定语,修饰 mortar。

② Eddystone Lighthouse 涡石灯塔耸立在离英格兰普利茅斯14英里的英吉利海峡中涡石礁上的灯塔,完全用联结的石块砌成,是灯塔建筑上的一次革命。

③ 动名词短语 burning the mixture 和 grinding the clinkers 与 proportioning limestone 一样是 method 的并列定语。

Exercises

Reading Comprehension

Ⅰ. Choose the most suitable alternative to complete the following sentences.

1. The stability of the earliest stone structures depended on _____.

    A. a volcanic tuff

    B. the use of mortar

    C. the regular setting of the heavy stones

D. the moist mud

2. The cementing material used in construction of some of the pyramids was _____.

    A. quicklime

    B. fine soil or earth

    C. a certain type of mineral admixture

    D. burnt gypsum

3. The cause that led to unstable properties of the natural cement was _____.

    A. the high temperature to burn the mixture

    B. variations in the proportions in the natural material

    C. the lime mixed with clay

    D. the gypsum used was not pure enough

4. The reason why Portland cement was so called was that _____.

    A. it was produced near Portland, England

    B. it was made by a brickmason in Portland, England

    C. it was made from a material taken from Portland, England

    D. the material used to make concrete resembled the limestone taken from Portland, England

5. Before Duff Abrams revealed the result of his research and observations, _____.

    A. reinforced concrete with steel rods had been widely used in European countries

    B. the concrete contained barely enough water to enable it to be rammed into place by the application of much hand labor

    C. the concrete was forced into place

    D. Both B and C

II. From the list below choose the most appropriate headings for each of the paragraphs in the text, then put the paragraph numbers in the brackets.

   A. Shipping artificial cement to the United States   (   )
   B. The skill of making cement material in the Middle Ages   (   )
   C. Construction of the structures in the earliest ages   (   )
   D. The use of concrete and the factor affecting the quality of concrete   (   )
   E. Joseph Aspdin and his method of producing Portland cement   (   )
   F. Cementing materials used by Egyptians, Greeks and Romans   (   )
   G. One discovery of making artificial cement   (   )
   H. The cause of natural cement production in the United States   (   )
   I. Hydraulic cement   (   )
   J. John Smeaton and the New Eddystone Lighthouse   (   )

III. Complete the following sentences with the information given in the text.

   1. In the earliest ages, structures consisted of _____, or _____.

   2. Greeks and Romans learned that fine _____, when mixed with _____ produced a superior _____.

3. Hydraulic cement means that the cement _____.
4. Joseph Aspdin's process of producing Portland cement consists of three steps. They are:
   1) _____.
   2) _____.
   3) _____.
5. The basic law of concrete technology is that _____ ; _____.

Vocabulary

I. Choose one word or expression which is the most similar in meaning to the word underlined in the given sentence.
   1. Compared with the first boy, the second one still has some capability for improvement.
      A. skill   B. ability   C. quality   D. intellegence
   2. The property of this metal is very erratic because of its active elements.
      A. irregular   B. common   C. unique   D. changeable
   3. The archaeologists discovered a lot of valuable objects from the vicinity of the hills of Thebes.
      A. surroundings   B. suburbs   C. scene   D. sides
   4. The inventor was informed that his patent would run out in two years' time.
      A. copyright   B. trademark   C. licence   D. certificate of invention
   5. Alcohol is often used as an admixture in some chemicals.
      A. a combination   B. a substance   C. a blend   D. something added

II. Match the words in Column A with their corresponding definitions or explanations in Column B

   A   B
   1. mortar   a. to change lime chemically by adding water
   2. clinker   b. to cause a solid to become liquid by putting into liquid
   3. gypsum   c. a mixture of lime, sand and water used to hold bricks, stone together in building a house
   4. quarry   d. a grey powder made from a burned mixture of lime and clay, which becomes hard like stone after having been mixed with water and allowed to dry
   5. slake   e. waste material left when coal or ore is burnt
                        f. a chalk-like substance used as a building material
                        g. to dig out or take sand, stone, etc.

h. to bring out the economic possibilities of land or natural substances

Reading Material A

The Hydration Reaction

　　In order to lead to a better understanding of the water-cement ratio, we should first examine and understand the reaction that takes place when Portland cement comes in contact with water. The reaction is called hydration, which is defined as the process of reacting with water to form new compounds.

　　When cement and water first come together they become a paste. It is this paste that binds the particles of aggregate together to form concrete. Every particle, from the smallest grain of sand to the largest stone, must be coated with this paste. After an initial period in a plastic condition the paste starts to stiffen or set, after several hours reaching a condition in which the paste completely loses its plasticity. If the paste is disturbed after it reaches this point, it will be seriously damaged.

　　The initial setting time is an arbitrary period of time measured from the time water and cement are combined until a small pat of cement paste will just support a certain size and weight of steel needle. Final set is determined with a heavier and larger needle.

　　The rate of setting is not necessarily the same as the rate of hardening. A high early strength cement can have nearly the same setting times as a common Type I cement, but it develops strength much more rapidly, once it has set.

　　Composition of Portland Cement. Cement is a complex mixture of several compounds that react with water. All of the compounds are anhydrous; that is, they are completely devoid of water. When brought into contact with water they actively react with the water, forming new hydrated compounds.① These hydration compounds are all of low solubility which gives concrete its durability.

　　Because of its complexity, cement cannot be shown by a simple chemical formula. Instead, a cement analysis report will show the amounts of all constituents of the cement.

　　Mechanism of Hydration. At the instant cement comes in contact with water the hydration reaction begins.② This reaction can continue for years. The rate of hydration is affected by the composition of the cement, fineness of the cement, temperature, the amount of water present, and the presence of admixtures. By varying the relative proportions of the compounds comprising the cement, the manufacturer can alter the rate at which the cement develops strength.③

　　A fine-ground cement will hydrate more rapidly than a coarse cement, merely because the smaller particles permit the water to penetrate into the particles faster. As in most chemical reactions, hydration of cement is accelerated under higher temperatures. At a temperature close to freezing of water, the reaction practically stops. High-temperature curing of concrete is practiced in products plant and casting yards to speed up the development of strength.

Water must be available for the hydration to continue. The process of hardening and strength development of concrete is not a process of drying out. If the concrete dries out completely, the reaction stops; however, it will recommence at a reduced rate if the concrete is again wetted.

Heat of Hydration. The reaction of cement and water is exothermic; that is, heat is generated during the reaction. Depending on the kind of structure in which the concrete is being used, this heat can be an advantage or disadvantage. In ordinary construction, members are of such size that release of this heat is no problem. In dams and other massive structures, means must be taken to reduce the rate of heat liberation by modifying the composition of the cement or by special design and construction provisions to remove it.④ By insulating the forms during cold weather the heat can be used to advantage to protect the concrete from freezing until it develops sufficient strength to withstand freezing.

Notes

①这些化合物一和水接触，它们就与水快速反应，生成新的水合化合物。
②当水泥与水相接触的瞬间，水合反应开始。
③水泥生产者可通过改变水泥成分的相对比例使水泥强度的增长率不同。
④在水坝和其它大型建筑工程中，必须采取措施，通过改变水泥的成分来降低其放热率，或者采用特殊的设计与施工措施将其消除掉。

Reading Material B

Distress and Failure of Concrete

Concrete and mortar are the only construction materials that are made on the site. Though subject to all the variations in weather, materials and methods, concrete under proper conditions of design, construction and control is nevertheless one of our most dependable and versatile construction materials, finding use in practically all types of construction, from the small family residence, high-rise buildings, highways, dams and other monumental works.①

As in all materials, problems sometimes arise and we find concrete that has failed to perform as expected. The distress and failure suffered by concrete is no accident; failures do not just happen, they are caused. Somewhere along the line someone, through ignorance, carelessness, or the misguided hope of saving a few cents, created or permitted a condition that led to the distress or failure. The distress that we see being suffered by concrete is a symptom, or group of symptoms, indicating that there is something wrong someplace. ② In some cases all we can do is remove or cover up the symptom, as we do when we take aspirin to stop a headache. ③ In other cases, we can root out the basic trouble, thus eliminating the cause of the symptom, as we do when we have an appendix removed, or treat any sickness.

So it is with concrete. ④ Sometimes all we can do, for instance, is patch the cracks, thus covering up the symptom, on the other hand, we can avoid crackinducing conditions or materials in the first place, thus preventing the basic trouble that shows up later as cracking. ⑤

Unfortunately, the cause of distress can rately be traced to one single factor, the distress usually resulting from several contributing causes. Broadly speaking, distress is caused by unsuitable materials, improper workmanship or the environment.

The first step in treatment of concrete that shows damage or deterioration is to classify the damage. This classification will assist in diagnosis, as forces that produce each kind of damage can be generalized, thus narrowing the field of possible aggressors. After this classification the cause may then be determined. This process of diagnosis may be quite simple and almost automatic, or it may involve a complicated and intensive job of detective work before the basic causes are found. Sometimes what seems to be the obvious cause is not the cause after all, or it may be one of several contributing to failure. The investigator should consider all facts that might be significant, such as determining the sources of materials used in construction, loading conditions, construction methods, design factors, conditions of exposure, presence of aggressive substances or forces, evidence of accidental damage, such as impact of vehicles, foundation conditions and others.

Once the cause has been isolated, corrective measures are taken. Such measures might include elimination of the cause, changes in the structure to enable it to withstand the destructive action, restoration of the damaged portions of the structure and protection to prevent further injury, abandonment of the structure and construction of a new one to withstand the action, or a combination of these.

Notes

①尽管天气，原材料，施工方法等各方面的变化会使混凝土遭受影响，然而在适当的设计，施工和管理条件下，它还是最可靠，用途最广的建筑材料之一。从小型家庭住宅到高层建筑、公路、水坝以及其它碑石工程，几乎在各种类型的建筑中它都得到应用。
②我们看到的混凝土所遭受的这种损坏是一种或一系列征兆，它暗示出某处存在某种毛病。
③在某些情况下所有我们能干的事就是清除或掩饰该症状，就像我们患头痛时吃阿斯匹林来止痛一样。
④对于混凝土来说也是如此。
⑤例如，有时候所有我们能够做的是修补裂缝，因而使症状掩盖起来。另一方面，我们可以在最初时就避免诱发裂缝的环境或材料，因而防止后来出现像裂缝那样基本的毛病。

UNIT TEN

Text   Advantages and Disadvantages of Concrete and Its Water-Cement Ratio

[1]　Concrete is a mixture of Portland cement, water, sand, and crushed gravel or stone. The water and cement form a cement paste in which the sand and stone or gravel are mixed. The sand and stone or gravel together make up the aggregate of a concrete mixture. The aggregate serves no structural function. It is merely a filler that adds low-cost bulk to the cement paste; it usually makes up about 75 percent of a given mass of concrete, by volume, although a poor aggregate can reduce the strength of a batch of concrete considerably, good aggregate adds only slightly to the strength of the cement.

[2]　The two principal advantages of concrete as a construction material are its relative cheapness and the ease with which it can be handled and placed while it is in the plastic state. The principal structural advantages of concrete are its great compressive strength and its durability. Concrete can withstand very high compressive loads. This is what makes concrete so suitable for the foundations, walls, and columns of buildings, and for driveways and walks as well.

[3]　The principal structural disadvantage of concrete is its poor tensile strength. That is, it cannot withstand pulling or bending loads without cracking or breaking. For this reason, steel rods, or reinforcement steel, are often embedded in concrete, the reinforcement steel providing the tensile strength the concrete lacks. Concrete with reinforcement steel embedded in it is reinforced concrete.

[4]　In addition to its poor tensile strength, concrete, like most construction materials, expands in hot weather and when wet and contracts in cold weather and as it dries out. Unless these movements are allowed for during construction, the concrete will crack.

[5]　And, contrary to common belief, solid concrete is not impervious to water. Some moisture will migrate into the best-made concrete. But if the concrete should be excessively porous, which can happen if too much water has been used in mixing it, moisture can easily enter the concrete after it has cured. If this moisture should be present within the concrete when cold weather comes, the moisture may freeze, which may result in serious frost damage to the structure.①

[6]　Despite these limitations, concrete is an inherently strong and durable construction material. If the proportions of water, cement, and aggregate are carefully calculated and if the concrete is placed and allowed to cure according to simple but definite rules, it is possible to obtain from the concrete all the strength and durability that is inherent in it.

[7]　The ratio of water to cement in a batch of concrete is the principal determinant of the concrete's final strength. At one time the instructions for preparing a batch of concrete would

have contained proportions such as 1∶2∶4, indicating that 1 part of Portland cement to 2 parts of sand to 4 parts of gravel by volume were to be mixed together, after which sufficient water was to be added to obtain a workable mixture. This procedure ignored entirely the importance of the water-cement ratio. It also resulted very often in the preparation of a very weak concrete, since the natural tendency is to add enough water to make placement of the concrete as easy as possible-the sloppier the better, as far as the workmen are concerned. This manner of specifying the proportions of concrete is obsolete and should never be followed.

[8]   In theory, it takes only 3 gal of water to hydrate completely 1 cu ft of cement. (A sack of cement contains 1 cu ft exactly, and the sack weighs 94 lb). But this water-cement ratio produces a mixture that is too stiff to be worked. In practice, therefore, additional water, between 4 and 8 gal per sack of cement, is used to obtain a workable mixture.

[9]   But the greater the proportion of water in a water-cement ratio, the weaker the final concrete will be. The additional water that is necessary to achieve a workable batch will only evaporate from the concrete as the concrete sets, and it will leave behind in the concrete innumerable voids. This is the reason there will always be some porosity in concrete. When an excessive amount of water has been used, there will be an excessive number of voids, which may cause the concrete to leak badly. If these voids should be filled with moisture when cold weather comes, they will cause the frost damage alluded to above.

[10]   As a general rule, therefore, 6 gal of water per sack of cement should be the maximum amount used for making concrete; and the less the amount of water that is used, the stronger the concrete will be. Also included in the 6 gal is whatever surface moisture is contained in the sand that is part of the aggregate.②

New Words and Expressions

gravel ['grævəl]	n.	砾石,砂砾
batch * [bætʃ]	n.	一批投料量
mass [mæs]	n.	块
durability [ˌdjuərə'biliti]	n.	耐久性,持久性
embed [im'bed]	vt.	把……嵌入,放入
impervious [im'pə:vjəs]	a.	不可渗透的,透不过的
migrate * ['maigreit]	vi.	移动,流动,迁移
cure * [kjuə]	vt.	养护(混凝土)
porous * ['pɔ:rəs]	a.	多孔的,有气孔的,能透水的
determinant [di'tə:minənt]	n.	决定因素,决定物
workable * ['wə:kəbl]	a.	有和易性的,可操作的
placement ['pleismənt]	n.	浇注,灌筑
sloppy ['slɔpi]	a.	湿透的,水多的,稀滑的

obsolete['ɔbsəliːt]	a.	已不用的,已废弃的	
gal[gæl]＝gallon	n.	加仑(1 gallon＝4.55 litres 公升)	
hydrate['haidreit]	vt.	使水合	
cu ft＝cubic foot		立方英尺	
lb＝pound(s)		磅 (1lb＝0.454 kg)	
void * [vɔid]	n.	孔隙,空洞,空隙	
porosity[pɔː'rɔsiti]	n.	孔隙度,多孔性	
allude[ə'ljuːd]	vi.	提及(to),提到	

Notes

① 本句中的 should 与上句中的 should 一样,在 if 所引导的条件句中表示语气较强的假设,意思为"一旦","万一"。关系代词 which 引导非限定性定语从句,修饰前面整个句子。

② 副词 also 和被动态过去分词 included 放在句首构成倒装句,其一起强调作用,其二,由于主语部分太长。倒装后能使句子保持平衡。其主语为由代词 whatever 所引导的主语从句。

Exercises

Reading Comprehension

Ⅰ. Choose the most suitable alternative to complete the following sentences.

1. The aggregate of concrete mixture consists of _____.

    A. Portland cement, water, sand and stone

    B. a cement paste, sand and gravel

    C. a cement paste and low-cost bulk

    D. sand and stone or crushed gravel

2. The reason why concrete is so suitable for the foundations, walls and columns of buildings is _____.

    A. its relative cheapness

    B. the ease with which it can be handled and placed while it is in the plastic state

    C. its great compressive strength and its durability

    D. its strong tensile strength

3. A common belief of people in solid concrete is that _____.

    A. some moisture will migrate into the best-made concrete

    B. using too much water will make concrete excessively porous

    C. the frozen moisture may result in serious frost damage to the structure

    D. solid concrete is impervious to water

4. The natural tendency to make concrete is _____.

   A. to add less water to make it stiff

   B. to add enough water to make placement of the concrete as easy as possible

   C. to take only 3 gal of water to hydrate completely 1 cu ft of cement

   D. to take 6 gal of water to hydrate completely 1 cu ft of cement

5. According to the author, the reason that causes concrete to leak badly is that _____.

   A. an excessive amount of water is used

   B. an insufficient amount of cement is used

   C. the concrete is frozen cracked

   D. innumerable voids remain inside the concrete when the additional water evaporates

II. From the list below choose the most appropriate headings for each of the paragraphs in the text, then put the paragraph numbers in the brackets.

   A. An inherently strong and durable construction material ( )

   B. Composition of concrete ( )

   C. Obsolete proportions of concrete ( )

   D. Moisture damage to the structure ( )

   E. Water-cement ratio in theory and in practice ( )

   F. The maximum amount of water used for making concrete ( )

   G. The principal structural disadvantages of concrete ( )

   H. The reason causing concrete to leak badly ( )

   I. Expansion and contraction of concrete ( )

   J. Two principal advantages of concrete ( )

III. Complete the following sentences with the information in the text.

   1. Concrete is a mixture of _____, _____, _____, _____, or _____.

   2. The principal structural advantages of concrete are its great _____ and its _____. And the principal disadvantage of concrete is it poor _____.

   3. If the _____ should be present _____ the concrete when _____ comes, the mosture _____, which may result in _____ to the structure.

   4. In practice, additional water between _____ and _____, is used to obtain a workable mixture.

   5. As a general rule, _____ of water _____ of cement should be _____ used for making concrete, and the _____ the amoumt of water that is used the _____ the concrete will be.

Vocabulary

I. Choose one word or expression which is most similar in meaning to the word underlined in the given sentence.

   1. All the remaining voids should be filled by progressively smaller sizes of sand and smaller

pieces of gravel.

　　A. gaps　　　　　B. breaks　　　　　C. openings　　　　D. empty space

2. Quartz sand is preferred because of its hardness and <u>durability</u>.

　　A. stability　　　B. reliability　　　C. endurance　　　D. firmness

3. The maximum size of the coarse <u>aggregate</u> in any particular mix depends mainly on the width of the forms into which the concrete is to be poured.

　　A. elements　　　B. materials　　　C. substances　　　D. compounds

4. If a <u>batch</u> of concrete works too easily and a film of water is brought to the surface, it is an indication of insufficient coarse aggregate.

　　A. measure　　　B. collection　　　C. volume　　　　D. quantity

5. After a concrete has been poured and has set, dispersed within every square inch of the concrete will be <u>innumerable</u> extremely small bubbles.

　　A. limitless　　　B. countless　　　C. endless　　　　D. measureless

II. Match the words in Column A with their corresponding definitions or explanations in column B.

A	B
1. embed	a. cause to take up or combine with water or the elements of water
2. obsolete	b. not allowing anything to pass through
3. allude	c. small stones with coarse sand used for roads and paths
4. gravel	d. no longer used; out of date
5. hydrate	e. to fix something firmly and deeply in a mass of surrounding matter
	f. the action of putting something in a position
	g. to join or fasten together
	h. to mention, to refer to

Reading Material A

Slump Test and Concrete Proportioning

A freshly mixed batch of concrete will slump if it is poured on a flat surface. Experience has shown that concretes having particular slumps are desirable for different types of structures. The amount of slump is thus a useful indication of the workability of the concrete while it is plastic and its potential strength when cured. The amount of slump is measured by a standardized slump test in which a truncated metal cone, 12 in high, is filled with a sample of the concrete. The concrete is tamped down solidly, the cone is raised, and the concrete will then slump. The amount of slump is then measured from the top of the truncated cone.

The amount of slump depends in part on the water-cement ratio (which is given and should not be changed), in part on the total proportion of aggregate in the mixture, and in part on the ratio between the fine and coarse aggregates in the mixture.

Ideally, the aggregate should range evenly in size from the largest pieces of gravel or stone to the smallest particles of sand. All the voids between the largest pieces of gravel should be filled by smaller pieces of gravel, and all the remaining voids should be filled by progressively smaller sizes of sand. In an ideal mix, only enough cement paste should be required to fill the voids left between all the particles of aggregate. Only then will one obtain the densest and strongest possible concrete mixture at the lowest possible cost. ①

On a large engineering project, the concrete can be especially formulated for the application. The physical characteristics of the fine and coarse aggregates can be ascertained and the exact proportions of water, cement, and coarse and fine aggregates can then be mixed together under closely controlled conditions to obtain the characteristics desired in the concrete, which are chiefly a specified 28-day compressive strength and a certain slump. ②

On a small job, however, such as the pouring of the foundations for a house, while it is easy enough to control the water cement ratio, it is not so easy to control either the particle sizes or the ratio of fine to coarse aggregate. Instead, one has to use what one has.

As for the water-cement ratio, one must remember to include as part of the ratio the water that has soaked into the sand pile. The amount of water in a pile of sand is easily estimated. If the sand is merely damp, the assumption is that the sand contains about 1/4 gal of water per cu ft. If the sand is wet (and most sands are wet), it will contain about 1/2 gal of water per cu ft. Very wet sand will contain at least 3/4 gal of water per cu ft and may contain as much as 1 1/4 gal if the sand is very finegrained. Whatever the moisture estimate, this quantity of water must be subtracted from the amount of water added separately to the mix. ③

As for the total amounts of fine and coarse aggregates required in a batch of concrete, the only way to proceed on a small job is by trial and error, as it is impossible to tell without physically segregating the particles just how evenly they are graded in the aggregate. ④ Practically, a builder can refer to some tables. They are useful primarily as guides, a builder will work up trial batches which he can then check by the slump test.

Attempting to increase the workability of a batch of concrete by adding more water is a very common and a very bad mistake. Not only is the original water-cement ratio upset, which will reduce the strength of the concrete, but a too-fluid mixture will allow the coarse aggregate to separate from the mix and settle to the bottom of the form. ⑤ This segregation of the coarse aggregate is one of the main causes of porous concrete that cracks easily and leaks badly.

Notes

①这时候才能以最低的成本消耗获得最大密度和最高强度的混凝土拌合物。

②先确定粗、细骨料的物理性能，然后在严密的控制下将比例精确的水、水泥和粗、细骨

料拌合在一起以获得混凝土的预期性能。这些性能主要是规定的二十八天抗压强度和某一确定的塌落度。

③无论砂子中所含的水分估计值有多大，这部分含水量都必须从单独加入到拌合料里的加水量中减去。

④至于一项小工程，一批量混凝土所需的粗、细骨料的总量只能通过反复摸索来确定。因为在没有完全将颗粒分开的情况下，不可能说出它们是如何按等级在骨料中均匀分布的。

⑤这不仅破坏了原来的水灰比，使该混凝土的强度降低，而且太稀的拌合料会使粗骨料从混合料中分离开，沉积到模板的底部。

Reading Material B

Curing Concrete

When a batch of concrete is first mixed, it forms a plastic mass that can be poured into prepared forms with little effort. In about an hour the concrete sets into a rigid mass that weighs about 150 lb per cu ft. The cement paste is said to hydrate, that is, the individual particles of cement absorb the surrounding molecules of water into their molecular structures. As they do, the cement crystallizes into a kind of rigid gel, something like gelatine, that gradually changes with the passing of time into a solid mass of minute, interlocked crystals. The longer hydration continues, the stronger the concrete will become. It is standard engineering practice, therefore, to calculate the final design strength of concrete on the basis of a 28-day curing period, although under exceptional conditions concrete has been known to continue increasing in strength for a quarter of a century and longer.①

The time during which concrete hydrates and increases in strength is its curing period. Concrete cannot hydrate, or cure, unless there is water present within the concrete. Throughout the curing period, therefore, all the exposed surfaces of the concrete must be kept moist. As long as the concrete is kept moist, curing will continue and the concrete will become increasingly stronger, denser, and more impervious to water.②

Once concrete is allowed to dry out completely, however, hydration stops. Usually it is the surface of concrete that is adversely affected by a too-short curing period. For example, the surface of a sample of concrete that has been kept moist for 28 days will be twice as strong as a surface that has been kept moist for only 3 days.

The outside air temperature is an extremely important factor in proper curing. If the air temperature is too high, over 90°F, say, the water in the concrete may evaporate away before hydration can be completed. An excessive internal temperature may also interfere with proper hydration. Concrete that has been mixed and placed during very hot weather is never as strong as concrete that has been placed when the air temperatures are 70°F and below, mainly because of the difficulty of keeping the concrete properly moist. Futhermore, concrete that sets too quickly during hot weather is more likely to crack afterward because it will have shrunk an excessive amount during is curing, and it will not thereafter be able to withstand the stresses imposed on it by large changes in temperature. ③

Nor can concrete be placed during freezing weather unless special precautions are taken to keep the concrete above 50°F for at least 4 days after it has been placed. If the temperature of the concrete should fall below 50°F, it will never harden properly. And if the concrete is allowed to freeze before it has set, it will be permanently damaged.

To cure concrete properly, the exposed surfaces must be kept continually moist from the moment the concrete first begins to set. The concrete must thereafter be kept continually moist for a minimum of 14 days, and longer if at all possible.

The simplest method of keeping concrete moist is to spray the surface with water at frequent intervals. Sand or burlap can be spread over the surface to help retain moisture. A covering is necessary, in any case, for the first 3 days after placing to protect the concrete from the direct rays of the sun.

Special curing compounds can also be sprayed on the concrete. The spraying should take place as soon as the surface of the concrete has lost its watery appearance. Properly applied, a curing compound will allow the concrete to continue curing even after the concrete has been placed in service, as with a concrete highway, for example. ④ Spraying on a curing compound is often the only practical method of curing concrete that has been poured into as unusual shape.

A third method of curing concrete is to spread a sheet of polyethylene film or building paper over the surface of the concrete. The polyethylene or building paper should overlap the sides of the exposed concrete. If several sheets of film or paper must be laid down to cover the concrete, the sheets should overlap by at lest 12 in., and the edges of the sheets should also be weighed down in some way. This covering must remain on top of the concrete for the entire curing period.

Notes

①因此，工程实践标准以二十八天养护期为准来计算混凝土的最终设计强度，尽管人们所熟知，在特殊条件下混凝土强度会不断增长可达二十五年或更长的时间。

②只要混凝土保持潮湿，养护将会不断继续，同时该混凝土会变得越来越坚固、密实、不透水。

③此外，由于在养护期内产生了超量的收缩，热天里固化的混凝土过后很可能开裂，而且它以后将不能承受由于大的温度变化而引起的、施加于它的应力。

④如果养护剂应用得当，它会使混凝土继续养护，即使已浇注完并已投入使用的混凝土也会如此，例如一条用混凝土浇筑的公路。

UNIT ELEVEN

Text   Mortar

[1]　　Mortar is a mixture of a cementitious material (which may be portland cement or lime or both) and sand. When water is added to these ingredients, the result is a plastic substance that is used to bind together bricks, tiles, concrete blocks, and other kinds of masonry units. After the mortar has set, the masonry units are bound together by the mortar in such a way that they form a single structural unit.

[2]　　Mortar is closely related to other cementitious materials such as concrete, plaster, and stucco, but it would be a mistake to confuse mortar with these other materials or attempt to use them as a substitute for mortar; the properties required of each are distinctive and differ from the others.

[3]　　By a mistaken analogy with a chain and its weakest link, it is a common belief that for any masonry construction to be strong, the mortar must be strong also. Very often, for example, a person who is familiar with concrete will infer that mortar, being a cementitious material like concrete, should have properties similar to those of concrete and be mixed and used in much the same way. ① Since, for example, concrete has, or should have, a high compressive strength, mortar should have a high compressive strength also. But the primary function of mortar is to bind the masonry units together, not to resist compressive loads or add to the strength of the masonry units.

[4]　　A great many tests have been made of brick walls built with mortars having a wide range of strength characteristics. ② These tests show uniformly that a brick wall is strongest when the mortar used to bind the brick is weaker than the brick. Indeed, the mortar can be substantially weaker than the brick without much affecting the overall strength of the construction. As long as the mortar is strong enough to resist the erosive effects of the weather and of freezing water, it is strong enough for use in the ordinary exterior wall.

[5]　　But suppose for the sake of argument that a brick wall has been built using a mortar that does have a compressive strength greater than that of the brick. ③Any stress this wall may be subjected to-the result of the settlement of the soil under the wall, say-will cause the brick to fracture along the line of greatest stress. This fracture will run in a single jagged crack right through the brick, from the top of the wall to the bottom.

[6]　　But when the mortar is weaker than the brick, as it should be, any stresses in the construction will be absorbed entirely by the mortar. The mortar will absorb these stresses in the form of a multitude of minute cracks invisible to the eye that leaves the basic strength of the construction unimpaired. The overall appearance of the wall and its structural integrity will be unchanged.

[7]　　Masonry constructions can, however, suffer from another type of failure. Sometimes

stresses are relieved by a separation of the mortar from the brick. The result is a zig-zag crack through the mortar that follows the brick pattern. What has happened here is that the bond between the brick and the mortar was too weak, a consequence either of ignorance or poor workmanship, or both, since the last thing that should happen in a well-made masonry wall is for there to be a poor bond between the masonry units and the mortar.④ Either the mortar was incorrectly proportioned and mixed or it was improperly applied to the brick, or both.

[8]   Freshly prepared mortar in which the cement, lime, and sand are accurately proportioned and mixed with the required amount of water has a quality called workability or, sometimes, plasticity. Workability is as difficult to describe in words as the consistency of pancake batter or soft butter, but fresh mortar that doesn't have this quality will be incapable of bonding masonry units together as tightly as they should be. A workable mortar can be spread with a trowel smoothly, evenly, and without effort. The mortar has a cohesive quality that enables it to hold its shape and keeps it from falling of its own weight when it is troweled onto the side of a brick. A workable mortar has a give to it that enables a bricklayer to bed masonry units solidly into place. One can say that on a microscopic scale a workable mortar makes such intimate contact with the surface of a masonry unit that the bond between the mortar and the masonry unit is as strong as possible.

New Words and Expressions

cementitious [simen'tiʃəs]	a.	(有)粘结性的
tile[tail]	n.	瓦片
masonry unit		砌块
stucco['stʌkəu]	n.	灰泥
analogy * [ə'nælədʒi]	n.	相似;类推
substantially[səb'stænʃəli]	ad.	大量地
erosive * [i'rəusiv]	a.	腐蚀(性)的
jagged['dʒægid]	a.	锯齿状的,参差不齐的
multitude * ['mʌltitju:d]	n.	许多,大批
unimpaired['ʌnim'pɛəd]	a.	未受损伤的
zig-zag['zigzæg]	a.	锯齿形的;之(Z)字形的
workability[wə:kə'biliti]	n.	和易性
consistency * [kən'sistənsi]	n.	稠度,浓度
pancake['pænkeik]	n.	薄煎饼
batter['bætə]	n.	(做糕饼时用面粉、鸡蛋等调成的)糊状物
trowel['trauəl]	n.	瓦刀
bricklayer['brikleiə]	n.	泥(瓦)工
cohesive[kəu'hi:siv]	a.	粘结的,粘性的,内聚的
solidly['sɔlidli]	ad.	紧密地,坚固地

give[giv]　　　　　　　　　　 *n.*　　 弹性

Notes

① 现在分词短语 being a cementitious…做定语,修饰 mortar。
② …with mortars having…是 with+*n.*+*v*-ing 组成的独立主格结构,做过去分词 built 的状语。
③ …that a brick wall…是 argument 的同位语从句;that does have…是 mortar 的定语从句。
④ What has happened…是主语从句;…there to be…做介词 for 的宾语。

Exercises

Reading Comprehension

Ⅰ. Choose the most suitable alternative to complete the following sentences.

1. It would be acceptable to _____.
   A. replace mortar with other cementitious materials
   B. distinguish mortar and other cementitious materials
   C. confuse mortar with concrete, plaster and stucco
   D. mix mortar with other cementitious materials

2. A lot of tests have been made in order to examine _____.
   A. the brick wall
   B. the lime
   C. the mortar
   D. portland cement

3. Any stress the wall may experience will lead to _____.
   A. a brick fracture along the line of the greatest stress
   B. the settlement of the soil under the wall
   C. a single jagged crack
   D. a compressive strength

4. Another failure suffered by masonry constructions has resulted from _____.
   A. the relief of stress
   B. a zig-zag crack
   C. a seperation of the mortar from the brick
   D. the very weak bond between the brick and the mortar

5. Fresh mortar with the quality of workability will _____.
   A. keep it from falling due to its own weight
   B. put bricks into place

C. be able to bond masonry units together tightly
D. be hard to describe in words

II. From the list below choose the most appropriate headings for each of the paragraphs in the text, then put the paragraph numbers in the brackets.

A. Test of mortar (　)
B. Mortar and other cementitious materials (　)
C. Mortar with weaker strength (　)
D. A false idea (　)
E. The definition of mortar (　)
F. Workability of mortar (　)
G. Mortar with greater compressive strength (　)
H. Another failure (　)

III. Complete the following sentences with the information given in the text.

1. Mortar is a _____ of _____ and _____.
2. After the mortar _____, the masonry units _____ by the mortar in such a way that _____.
3. But the primary function of mortar is to _____, not to _____ or _____.
4. Sometimes stresses are relieved by _____.
5. A workable mortar can be spread with _____ and _____.

Vocabulary

I. Choose one word or expression which is the most similar in meaning to the word underlined in the given sentence.

1. To make this cake you must first mix the flour and milk to the right <u>consistency</u>.
   A. richness   B. dampness   C. thickness   D. density
2. A <u>multitude</u> of football fans assembled in the stadium.
   A. plenty   B. multiple   C. lot   D. quantity
3. There is <u>an analogy</u> between the way water moves in waves and the light travels.
   A. an imitation   B. a comparison   C. an equality   D. a resemblance
4. The money you gave me helped <u>substantially</u> towards paying for our education.
   A. absolutely   B. considerably   C. hugely   D. bulkily
5. Flour and sugar are the most important <u>ingredients</u> to make a cake.
   A. elements   B. mixtures   C. divisions   D. shares

II. Match the words in Column A with their corresponding definitions or explanations in Column B.

A	B
1. stucco	a. loose material of very fine grains
2. tile	b. a mix of lime, sand and water used in building
3. cohesive	c. a tool with a flat blade for speading cement
4. trowel	d. material (plaster) used on buildings to cover walls
5. jagged	e. a thin shaped piece of baked clay used for covering roofs, walls, floors etc.
	f. tending to stick together
	g. having a rough, uneven edge
	h. a piece of cloth used for drying wet skin etc.

Reading Material A

Water Retentivity

The ability to retain its water content is another quality of freshly mixed mortar that is closely related to workability. A mortar that has good water retentivity is not only workable, it will also retain its workability for a considerable period of time. The water does not evaporate too quickly from the mortar if it should be exposed to the air, nor is the water sucked too easily from the mortar by dry, porous masonry units.

What happens if mortar having poor water retentivity is used to build a brick wall?① The bricklayer first lays down a line of mortar on which he beds the first course of brick.② After the first course is in place, he spreads mortar over the brick preparatory to laying the second course. If the brick is porous and the mortar has poor water retentivity, the brick in the first course will have sucked the water from the mortar, and the mortar will have stiffened considerably before the second course of brick can be laid in place. As a result, the second course of brick cannot be bedded securely in place and the bond between the mortar and the brick will not be strong.

In addition, as the wall is built higher and higher, the brick in the lower courses will not be able to adjust themselves to the stresses imposed upon them by the weight of the brick above.③ The entire wall, therefore, although it certainly won't collapse, will be poorly bonded together. In time, large cracks will undoubtedly open up in the mortar joints, resulting in the zig-zag appearance described above. In addition, in rainy weather the entire construction will leak, and if the weather is cold any moisture that makes its way into the cracks will freeze and gradually cause the mortar to erode away.

This sort of problem can be prevented by using a mortar that has good water retentivity. And how is good water retentivity obtained? By making the mortar with well-graded sand and by using lime in the mortar. Water retentivity can also be increased by adding an air-entrainment chemical to the mortar, as described below. Finally, if the brick is too porous, their porosity can be reduced by soaking them with water beforehand.

The water retentivity of a batch of mortar can be tested on a flow table similar to that used to test the consistency of mortar. The difference is that when testing for water retentivity the plate has small holes drilled through its surface, these holes being connected to a vacuum pump. The cone-shaped pile of mortar is placed on the table as already described and allowed to spread under vibration. A consistency measurement is then taken. The mortar is then subjected to a controlled amount of suction to draw out some of its water content. The mortar is then repacked into the truncated cone and the consistency test is repeated. The second time around the mortar will not spread as readily as it did the first time because of the loss of some of its water. The difference between the two consistency measurements, expressed as a percent, is an indication of how well the mortar was able to retain its water. If, for example, the mortar had a consistency of 100 percent before being subjected to suction and a consistency of 80 percent afterward, then its water retentivity would be $80/100 \times 100$ percent $= 80$ percent.

In practice, it has been found that a mortar having a water retentivity of 85 percent is the most workable, although mortars with water retentivities as low as 70 percent are acceptable.④ The greater the amount of water retained, the better, as long as the mortar does not have so much water in it that it turns loose and sloppy.⑤

Mortars are classified as either cement mortars, cement-lime mortars, or lime mortars. All three types are mixed with sand, the primary purpose of which is to reduce to a minimum the shrinkage that occurs in cement and lime as they set.

Both portland cement and lime bind masonry units together as follows. When the cement or lime hardens, it does so in the form of a dense network of microscopic-sized interlocking crystals. It is this interlocking, crystalline structure of cement and lime that gives them their strength in the first place. When these crystals interlock with the minute crevices, protuberances, and voids that lie exposed on the surface of a brick, the result is a strong bond between the two.⑥

Notes

①如果用保水性较差的砂浆砌筑砖墙会怎样呢？
②首先泥瓦工抹上一层砂浆，然后在砂浆上砌筑第一层砖。
③此外，由于墙越建越高，底层的砖无法适应上面的砖的重量所施于它们的压力。
④实际上，人们发现，尽管低达70％保水性的砂浆是合格的，但具有85％保水性的砂浆最具和易性。
⑤只要砂浆所含的水量不使其过于流动稀薄，那么，水的含量越高越好。
⑥当这些晶粒与位于砖面上微小的裂缝、突起物和孔隙互相结合时，其结果是双方的粘结极强。

Reading Material B

Cement Mortar and Lime Mortar

The ordinary Types I, II and III portland cements that are used to make concrete are also used to make mortar. The only difference between a portland-cement mortar and a portland-cement concrete is that the concrete contains a coarse aggregate consisting of large stones and gravel in addition to sand, while the mortar contains only sand. ①

The great defect of a mortar that is made entirely from portland cement is that when the mortar is mixed to achieve the maximum possible amount of strength, it will be too stiff to be workable or bond tightly to the masonry units. On the other hand, when a portland-cement mortar is mixed so that it is workable, it will contain so much water that it will be unable to develop its full strength.

An all-portland-cement mortar does have its place in construction, however, and this is where exceptionally strong brick is being used to construct a foundation wall, or when a foundation wall will be subjected to a hydrostatic pressure. Under these conditions, the strength of the mortar and its imperviousness to water penetration are valuable attributes. If, however, an all-portland-cement mortar is used with brick or concrete blocks having ordinary strengths, the mortar may be so strong that the masonry units will crack instead of the mortar if the construction is stressed excessively.

All-lime mortars are of great antiquity and were used by both the Greeks and Romans in exactly the same way as they were until quite recent times. There are many Roman-built brick and stone structures that are still standing in which the mortar joints are as solid as ever, 2000 years after these structures were completed. ②

Lime is made from calcium carbonate or a combination of calcium and magnesium carbonates. The carbonates are crushed and heated in a kiln to drive off their chemically bound water. The resultant product is called quicklime. In order that quicklime can be used as a mortar, it must first be slaked, which means water is added to it to form the compound calcium hydroxide, which, when it has an excess of water, forms a slurry called lime putty. ③ This lime putty can rest for a considerable period of time before it is used. Indeed, the longer it rests the more plastic and workable it will become, and the better a mortar it will make. In times past it was not unusual to rest lime putty for 10 weeks and more before using it. This is the way that the Greeks and Romans prepared their lime mortars. That their structures have remained standing for so long a time is a tribute to the thoroughness with which they slaked and mixed their lime. ④

If, during the slaking of the quicklime, just enough water is added to form the calcium hydroxide without there being any surplus water left over, the result is a dry powder called hydrated lime. ⑤ Hydrated lime can be mixed with sand and water and used immediately, but the mortar will be greatly improved if the hydrated lime is mixed with water first and this mixture is allowed to rest for about 24 hr before it is used.

The great disadvantage of lime mortars is that they take a considerable time to set hard, since their setting depends on a recombination of the lime with the carbon dioxide in the atmosphere to form the original carbonate again.

Notes

①硅酸盐水泥砂浆与硅酸盐水泥混凝土的唯一不同是混凝土除有砂子外，还含有由大石块和砾石组成的粗骨料，而砂浆仅含有砂子。
②现在仍存有许多罗马时期建造的砖石结构，尽管已建成2000年了，但在这些结构中砂浆的粘结处仍坚固如初。
③为了能把生石灰当做砂浆使用，首先必须把它水解，也就是加入水后形成一种化合物氢氧化钙，这种化合物当含水量过多时就形成了一种称做石灰膏的稀灰浆。
④他们的建筑年代久远是对他们水解和混合石灰完善性的一种赞颂。
⑤在水解生石灰的过程中，如果加入适量的水形成氢氧化钙，且没有多余的水遗留下来，其结果就形成了一种叫做熟石灰的干粉。

UNIT TWELVE

Text   General Planning Considerations

[1]   The selection of a high-rise building structure is not based merely on understanding the structure in its own context. The selection may be more function of factors related to cultural, social, economical and technological needs.① One should keep in mind that structure is just one important consideration among many. Some of the factors related primarily to the technological planning of high-rise buildings are discussed next.

[2]   The architect is usually obliged to respond to the purpose of many building types: to make money. As he forms a better understanding of the economic aspects of the design process, he may improve his chance of creating better architecture.

[3]   The important point to realize is that a building system should not just be a preconceived preference; rather, it should incorporate careful consideration of economic factors.② Thus two or more different methods of construction may hold up a particular building and may even look very similar, but one system usually is more economical to build.

[4]   A designer must think not only about how much the project costs to build but also about how much the finished project costs to operate; he has to deal with the building economy. As the height of the building increases, more and more space is needed for structure, mechanical systems, and elevators, leaving less rental space. In addition, the costs of elevators and mechanical systems increase with height. The same reasoning applies to contractor costs, since more sophisticated construction equipment is necessary as buildings get taller. However, all these cost increases may be offset by the high land costs and the need for the building at a specific location. As the building height increases, the land costs per square foot of floor area obviously decrease. Similarly, management costs are reduced, since it costs less per square foot to operate one large building than several small structures.

[5]   Accurate evaluation of all the complex economic considerations for high-rise buildings has come to depend on the computer. It is beyond human calculation to decipher all the factors along with all the ramifications of each factor concerned with the skyscrapers of today.

[6]   The coordination of architect, engineer and contractor during a project's planning and drawing stage will improve the potential of achieving an economical solution. Such team efforts may allow building construction to start before all final drawings are completed. When construction begins earlier, buildings save money on inflating construction prices and earn profits sooner.

[7]   The performance of a building is dependent on the strength of the soil on which it is founded. The foundation or substructure binds the superstructure to the soil. It receives its loads and distributes them so that the soil is capable of carrying them. The selection of the building type is very much a function of the geology of the site. The soil conditions must be ex-

plored before any structural system can be decided on, so that its behavior can be predicted. If, for instance, the bearing capacity of the soil is rather low at a specific site, piles or caissons may be required to reach the proper foundation support. In this type of situation a building of heavy materials such as concrete may be much more expensive than lightweight steel construction. In any case, the three building structure variables—superstructure, substructure, and soil—leave some combinational freedom with respect to choice of that structural system.

[8]　The planning of fabrication and erection procedures may indicate important factors concerning structural system selection. Indeed, these may be the governing considerations when choosing a prefabricated construction method. Such systems are used because they may reduce labor costs and time required for erection of buildings. There should be a minimum number of structural pieces to shorten construction time; complicated closed-form shapes should be avoided, and field welding should be minimized. Thus, before choosing a construction method, the fabrication and erection procedures must be known.

[9]　Mechanical systems, consisting of HVAC (heating, ventilating, and air conditioning), elevator, electric, plumbing, and waste disposal systems, average more than one-third of total high-rise building costs. This significant cost factor exemplifies clearly that the sturctural system selection must respond to these building services. Energy supply systems may be concentrated in mechanical cores integrated with a general core area, sometimes separate duct spaces are provided in the exterior facade, or interspatial systems with mechanical levels for heavy service requirements are used. All these approaches have definite effects on the overall building appearance and economic selection of a structural system.

New Words and Expressions

context * ['kɔntekst]	n.	上下文，情况
technological [teknə'lɔdʒikəl]	a.	技术的，工艺的
preconceived [ˌprikən'siːvd]	a.	事先想好的
rental ['rentl]	a.	租用的
	n.	租费
offset * ['ɔ(ː)fset]	vt.	抵销，补偿
decipher [di'saifə]	vt.	解释，译解
ramification [ˌræmifi'keiʃən]	n.	分枝，细节
inflating [in'fleitiŋ]	a.	膨胀的，抬高的
substructrue [sʌb'strʌktʃə]	n.	基础，下部结构
superstructure [ˌsjuːpə'strʌktʃə]	n.	上层建筑，上部结构
geology [dʒi'ɔlədʒi]	n.	地质学
caisson ['keisən]	n.	沉箱
combinational [ˌkɔmbi'neiʃənl]	a.	结合的，配合的
prefabricated [priˈfæbrikeitid]	a.	预制的

minimize * ['minimaiz]	v.	使减少到最少,使降到最低
ventilate * ['ventileit]	vt.	使通风,换气
exemplify * [ig'zemplifai]	vt.	举例说明
facade [fə'sa:d]	n.	正面,表面
interspatial [intə'speiʃəl]	a.	空间的
coordination [kəu,ɔ:di'neiʃən]	n.	配合,协调

Notes

① 此句中 related to cultural, … 为过去分词短语作定语,修饰 factors。
   be more function of 意为:更多地取决于……。

② …a building system should not just be a preconceived preference, rather, it should… 当 rather 作为副词位于否定句之后,另一句之首时,意思是"相反"。

Exercises

Reading Comprehension

Ⅰ. Choose the most suitable alternative to complete the following sentences.

1. According to the text, the selection of a structure should _____.
   A. be based only on understanding the structure itself
   B. be based on considerations of cultural, social, economical and technological needs
   C. be based on preconceived preference
   D. be based only on consideration of economic factors

2. As the building height increases, _____.
   A. more and more space is needed for structure, mechanical systems and elevators
   B. the land costs per square foot of floor area decrease
   C. management costs are reduced
   D. all the above

3. The computer is depended on because it is beyond human calculation _____
   A. to decipher the factors concerned with the skyscrapers
   B. to desipher all the ramifications of each factor
   C. to decipher all the factors together with all the ramifications of each factor
   D. to decipher all the costs

4. Before choosing a construction method, one must know
   A. the labor costs only
   B. the time required for erection first
   C. the fabrication and erection procedures

D. the fabrication procedures

5. If the bearing capacity of the soil is low at a specific site, _____.

   A. piles or caissons may be required to reach the foundation support
   B. heavy walls may be required to reach the foundation support
   C. buildings can be set up on it
   D. nothing can help

II. From the list below choose the most appropriate headings for each of the paragraphs in the text, then put the paragraph numbers in the brackets.

   A. The building economy considerations   (   )
   B. The purpose of building types   (   )
   C. The factors concerning the selection of a structure   (   )
   D. The computer   (   )
   E. Team efforts   (   )
   F. Soil conditions   (   )
   G. Fabrication and erection considerations   (   )
   H. Mechanical systems considerations   (   )
   I. An important point   (   )

III. Complete the following sentences with the information given in the text.

   1. Structure is _____ _____ of the important considerations.
   2. A better understanding of the _____ of the design process may help _____ a lot.
   3. The _____ of architect, engineer and contractor will improve _____.
   4. In the text, the three structural variables refer to _____, _____ and _____.
   5. All these approaches have definite effects on the overall building appearance and economic selection of a structural system. These approaches are:
      1) _____.
      2) _____.
      3) _____.

Vocabulary

I. Choose one word or expression which is the most similar in meaning to the word underlined in the given sentence.

   1. The selection of a high-rise building structure is not based merely on understanding the structure in its own <u>context</u>.
      A. connection   B. contents
      C. contain   D. conditions
   2. A building system should <u>incorporate</u> careful consideration of economic factors.
      A. organize   B. include
      C. combine   D. identify

3. It is imposible for us to decipher all the factors.

   A. explain   B. work

   C. solve   D. decide

4. All the cost increases may be offset by the high land costs.

   A. opposed   B. adjusted

   C. compensated D. satisfied

5. If construction begins earlier, buildings will save money on inflating construction prices and earn profits sooner.

   A. rising   B. extending

   C. advancing   D. lengthening

Ⅲ. Match the words in Column A with their corresponding definitions or explanations in Column B.

A	B
1. ramification	a. a branch of a system that has many parts
2. fabrication	b. a picture or plan in pencil, etc.
3. caisson	c. the act of making by putting parts together
4. duct	d. a large box put underground
5. pile	e. any kind of pipe in the ground or in a building for carrying liquids or other substances, or power lines
	f. the act of erecting
	g. a heavy wooden, metal or stonelike (concrete) post hammered upright into the ground as a support for a building, a bridge, etc.
	h. a set of wires put underground or under the sea which carry telegraph and telephone mesages

Reading Material A

Housing

Housing is the living quarters or human beings.① The basic function of housing is to provide shelter from the elements, but people today require much more than this of their housing.② A family moving into a new neighborhood will want to know if the available housing meets its standards of safety, health, and comfort. A family will also ask how near the housing is to churches, schools, stores, the library, a movie theater, and the community center.

In the mid-1960's a most important value in housing was sufficient space both inside and out. A majority of families preferred single-family homes on about half an acre of land, which would provide space for spare-time activities. Many families preferred to live as far out as possible from the center of a metropolitan area, even if the wage earners had to travel some distance to their work.③ About four out of ten families preferred country housing to suburban housing because their chief aim was to get far away from noise, crowding, and confusion. The accessibility of public transportation had ceased to be a decisive factor in housing because most workers drove their cars to work. People were chiefly interested in the arrangement and size of rooms and the number of bedrooms.

Types of Housing

The majority of residents in rural and suburban areas live in single-family dwellings. Housing developments containing many single-family units have been built by professional land developers.④ Levittown, N.Y., is a mass-produced development that contains homes for more than 60,000 people. Since they are mass-produced, development houses tend to be identical or very similar. For the same reason they are usually less expensive than houses that are individually built.

In crowded areas where land is fairly expensive, the semidetached, or two-family house is frequently found. In a semidetached house two dwellings share a center wall. Construction and heating are cheaper than in one-family houses, but residents have less privacy. Row houses, in which a number of single-family houses are connected by common walls on both sides, are still less expensive to build.

City land is too expensive to be used for small housing units, except in the upper price bracket.⑤ A more efficient type of building, which houses many families on a plot of ground that would hold only a few single-family units, is the multistory dwelling, or apartment house.⑥ Apartment houses may range from houses of only a few stories, without elevators, to structures of 20 or more stories, with several elevators. Some apartment houses offer city dwellers a terrace or a backyard, where they can grow a few plants or eat outdoors. Many apartment houses provide garage space, laundromats, and gardened foyers. Huge apartment developments may cover several square blocks and include parks, playgrounds, shops, and community centers.

Notes

①living quarters 可译为"住所"。
②elements 此处意为"风雨"或"自然力"。
③as far out as possible from 离……尽可能远。
④此句中 development 建筑区，建房区；
　　developer 开发人（指开发土地建造房屋以赢利者）。

⑤upper price brackets 高价档。

⑥此处 houses 为动词，译为"为……提供住房"。

Reading Material B

House

House is a building that provides home for one or more families. Its main function is to provide shelter, but a house usually serves many more purposes. It is a center of family activities, a place for entertaining friends, and a source of pride in its comfort and appearance.

Classification of houses

Many private houses built in the United States are designed by builders, rather than by architects. For this reason, houses are most easily identified by the type of layout or the floor plan, not by reference to architectural styles. Most houses can be described in terms of the following categories.

Cape Cod. The Cape Cod house is usually small and has a sharply sloping roof. Many Cape Cods have three or four rooms on the ground floor and two small rooms on the second floor. In the modified Cape Cod the second floor is made larger by decreasing the slope of the roof in the rear and by adding dormers, or gabled extensions with windows, in the front.① The Cape Cod originated in colonial New England.

Two-Story House. Before World War II the usual one-family house had two full stories, as well as a basement and an attic. This type of house is probably still the most common house, and many new ones are being built. It usually has a square floor plan and a central hall, and it is often called a Colonial house.

Ranch House. The ranch house is long and low, and all the rooms are at ground level. Some ranch houses have no basements. The ranch house originated in the West and Southwest and became popular in the building boom that followed World War II.②

Split-level House.③ The split-level has two or more levels, separated from each other by half flights of steps. The kitchen and family room may be on one level, The living room on a second level, and the bedrooms on a third level. This house was developed in the building boom that followed World War II, and it is probably the most popular type being built.

Attached Houses.④ Houses for two families are often called duplex houses, because they have two stories. One family may live on each story, or each family may have both upstairs rooms and downstairs rooms, with the two parts of the house separated by a wall through the middle.

In towns and cities there are often rows or two-story houses attached to each other. These are called row houses.⑤ Each unit in a row may be a one-family or two-family house.

Variation. There are a number of variations and combinations of the above basic styles.

An example is the raised ranch house. Like the ranch house, the raised ranch house has its main rooms on one level, but unlike the ranch house, this level is a second story. The lower floor usually contains a garage, a family room, and an extra bedroom.

The exterior of any of the above houses may be decorated in various architectural styles. The Colonial styles are the most popular.

Notes

①改良的科德房屋通过减缓后部屋顶的坡度并加开天窗，或者在房子前部延长有窗的山墙来增大二楼面积。
②牧场式房屋起源于美国西部和西南部，它是在第二次世界大战后的建筑兴盛时期流行起来的。
③split-level house　错综式房屋。
④attached houses　附联式房屋。
⑤row houses　联立房屋，行列式房屋。

UNIT THIRTEEN

Text   Factory Design

[1]   Factory design is interesting to most civil engineers because it includes the design of many important services, and the engineer is the main designer, not a mere helper as he is for a multi-storey building. He must design the roads and the drains, possibly the water supply and the heating or air conditioning and provide for the power and telephone cables and gas pipes. If possible he will try at least to get the main roads and drains in position before the main construction starts. [1] This will make the site much easier to travel over, and by keeping it drier will probably reduce the damage to vehicles.

[2]   Provided that a factory is of one storey,[2] it can usually be well lit from the roof except in hot climates, but if it is more than one storey high, day-lighting of the lower storeys in any large-span building becomes difficult or impossible. For this reason, some US factory designers have built factories without windows, entirely air-conditioned. And as spans increase this will become unavoidable for the internal rooms. In fact, it is now quite common to place bathrooms internally so that they do not waste the valuable space for windows that would be more useful to a living-room. In temperate climates, the air-conditioning equipment should be designed to provide cooled air in summer and warm air in winter.

[3]   Roof lighting can be through transparent sheets in an ordinary sheeted sloping roof, or through a sawtooth roof which would be north-facing in northern continents or south-facing in southern. A monitor roof enables the lights to be either vertical or on the roof slope and also provides excellent ventilation. Glass is still the commonest material used for admitting light because it is the cheapest, but in hot countries it is unsuitable. In a sheeted roof occasional sheets may be replaced with a translucent or transparent material, either glass fiber which is translucent, or one of the transparent plastics materials, which may be colourless or tinted red, yellow, etc. All these large sheets can be corrugated to allow them to span over distances of about 2 m.

[4]   Factory construction, the design and construction of single-storey buildings of large span often hundreds of metres long, is a typical task of the civil engineer. Though architects often supervise these projects, they succeed generally because the architect and the civil engineering designer work together, with understanding of the client's needs.

[5]   For light industry which is not noisy, the roofing and cladding generally consist of factory-made sheets, of which hundreds of types exist, made of corrugated or troughed or flat steel, plywood, aluminium, or asbestos-cement. The waterproof skin on the outside of some of them may also be of copper sheet, tarred felt or steel. Some of these cladding or roofing units are expensive, especially the sandwich units which contain a middle layer of highly efficient thermal insulator, such as expanded polystyrene or glass fibre.

[6]   The insulation must be completely protected from the condensation of water out of the

air from the hotter side of the cool insulating material. Thus in a hot climate the condensation will be on the inner face of the insulator and in a cold climate on its outer face. The insulation must be protected from moisture or it will rapidly lose its insulating power as the moisture enters it. As it loses insulating power, the condensation will increase, more moisture will enter and the insulation will be completely lost, quite apart from the unpleasantness of dampness in the wall.③

[7]　It is therefore essential to prevent not only moisture but also air from entering the insulation, and this is done by a waterproof sheet of polythene or metal or other material, called a vapour barrier. It must be sealed at the joints to prevent air leaking through and condensation occurring inside. The civil engineer should therefore ask whether the cladding is for use in a hot or a cold climate, and the maker will usually be happy to provide a possible buyer with all this information.

[8]　For noisy factories, such as those which house heavy industry (car factories, etc.), cladding sheets are not good because noise passes through them. Any heavy walling is better because the deadening of sound depends on the weight of the wall. Brickwork has been the universal material in Britain in the past but modern civil engineering contractors have precast large concrete units of 4 m—5 m and placed them with powerful cranes. Such walls are quickly built provided that the organization of the site is good, and the cranes are available and able to get to the lifting point. If the units are too large for one crane, they are sometimes lifted by two cranes working together. The alternative is to reduce the height of the wall unit, keeping its length equal to the column spacing, since this construction is simple and looks good. If the crane is very small and the units are only about 15 cm high, it may be advisable to lay a thin mortar joint between the units so as to keep out the wind. For the very large units, the mortar joint is less important since the joints are fewer.

New Words and Expressions

multi-storey['mʌlti'stɔːri]	n.	多层
unavoidable[ˌʌnə'vɔidəbl]	a.	不可避免的
temperate['tempərit]	a.	（气候等）温和的,适度的
translucent[trænz'ljuːsnt]	a.	半透明的
condensation[ˌkɔnden'seiʃn]	n.	冷凝,凝结
colorless['kʌləlis]	a.	无色的
tint[tint]	vt.	给……染色
corrugate['kɔrugeit]	v.	成波状,加工成波纹状
monitor['mɔnitə]	n.	采光顶,天窗
sawtooth['sɔːtuːθ]	n.	锯齿（形状）
supervise['sjuːpəvaiz]	v.	监督,管理

client[ˈklaiənt]	n.	委托人,当事人
clad * [klæd]	v.	在……包上另一层,覆盖
cladding[ˈklædiŋ]	n.	被覆,包层
troughed[trɔft]	a.	槽型的
plywood[ˈplaiwud]		胶合板
asbestos[æzˈbestɔs]	n.	石棉
asbestos-cement		石棉水泥板
tarred felt		油毡
ventilation[ventiˈleiʃn]	n.	通风,换气
sandwich[ˈsænwidʒ]	n.	夹层
thermal[ˈθəːməl]	a.	热的,热量的
polystyrene[pɔlisˈtaiəriːn]	n.	聚苯乙烯
insulator[ˈinsjuleitə]	n.	绝缘体
insulation[insjuˈleiʃn]	n.	绝缘,隔热层
insultate[ˈinsjuleit]	vt.	使绝缘
unpleasantness[ʌnˈplezəntnis]	n.	不愉快
dampness[ˈdæmpnis]	n.	潮湿
polythene[ˈpɔliθiːn]	n.	聚乙烯
vapour barrier		隔汽层
deadening of sound		消声
column spacing		柱间距(隔)

Notes

① If possible…是省略句,省略了 it is。

　　get sth in position 原意是"把……放在适当的位置,给……定位",…get the main roads and drains in position…可译为:把主要道路和排水管道铺设好。

② Provided that a factory is of one storey 句中 provided that 是连接词,译为"假设","如果"; is of one storey＝is one storey high 这种句型在此句中表示厂房高度。

③ …quite apart from the unpleasantness of dampness in the wall. 可译为:更不用说阻挡墙上令人讨厌的潮湿了。

Exercises

Reading Comprehension

I. Choose the most suitable alternative to complete the following sentences.

1. Most civil engineers are interested in factory design because _____.
   A. the engineer is the only designer
   B. it includes the design of many important services and the engineer is the main designer
   C. the engineer is the main helper of the design
   D. they may work together with the architect

2. Some U. S. factories are built without windows, entirely air-conditioned, because _____.
   A. air-conditioning is popular
   B. the climate is always hot in the U. S.
   C. in factories more than one story high, day-lighting of the lower storeys in any large-span building is difficult or impossiple
   D. dayt-lighting in any building is impossible

3. The most common material used for admitting light is _____
   A. transparent plastics
   B. glass fiber
   C. translucent plastics
   D. glass

4. The insulation must be protected from moisture or _____.
   A. it will rapidly lose its insulating power
   B. air will enter the hotter side of the room
   C. the condensation will be on the inner face of it
   D. the condensation will be on the outer face of it

5. In Britain, for noisy factories, brickwork has been replaced by _____.
   A. large precast concrete units of 4 m-5 m
   B. precast concrete units of 15 cm only
   C. cladding sheets
   D. precast concrete units with mortar joints only

II. From the list below choose the most appropriate headings for each of the paragraphs in the text, then put the paragraph numbers in the brackets.

   A. Factory lighting and air-conditioning   (   )
   B. The noisy factory walling   (   )
   C. A civil engineer's work in factory design   (   )

D. Factory construction (　　)
   E. The insulation (　　)
   F. The roofing and cladding of light industry (　　)
   G. Roof lighting (　　)
   H. A vapour barrier (　　)

III. Complete the following sentences with the information given in the text.
   1. It is now quite common to place bathrooms internally so as to _____.
   2. The roofing and cladding of light industry generally consist of factory-made sheets which are made of _____ or troughed or _____, _____, aluminiam, or _____.
   3. In a hot climate the condensation of water will be _____ of the insulator and in a cold climate _____.
   4. A vapour barrier is a waterproof sheet of _____ or _____ or _____.
   5. Provided that the organigation of the site is good and the cranes are available _____.

Vacabulary

I. Choose one word or expression which is the most similar in meaning to the word underlined in the given sentence.
   1. In temperate climates, air-conditioning is less popular than in hot climates.
      A. comfortable   B. cool
      C. moderate   D. clear
   2. A monitor roof may provide light as well as ventilation.
      A. circulating   B. dicussing
      C. expressing   D. airing
   3. Glass is still widely used for admitting light because it is the cheapest.
      A. letting in   B. allowing of
      C. agreeing to   D. taking on
   4. For noisy factories such as those which house heavy industry, cladding sheets are not good because noise passes through them.
      A. lodge   B. remain
      C. dwell   D. contain
   5. Any heavy walling is better because the deadening of sound depends on the weight of the wall.
      A. dying   B. reducing
      C. disppearing   D. relieving

II. Match the words in Column A with their corresponding definitions or explanations in Column B.

109

A	B
1. a monitor roof	a. a structural material consisting of sheets of wood glued or cemented together
2. span	b. the distance between two extremities
3. sandwich	c. the place where two things or more are joined
4. plywood	d. a raised central portion of a roof having low windows for providing light or air
5. joint	e. sth. put in between two other things
	f. the outside covering on top of a building
	g. a movable flat surface that opens and closes the entrance to a building, room, etc.
	h. opening in wall or roof of building, ship, etc.

Reading Material A

Modern Building Construction

Before any building project can be undertaken, numerous decisions must be made. The design program must be resolved. The site must be chosen and economic feasibility determined.① Finally, a completed design for the building must be made. Each of these elements is important; none can be considered in isolation of the others.

Frequently a decision is made to construct a building before much has been determined about its function.② In the case of a residence, little information is needed to make the decision to build. In the case of other buildings, such as offices or retail stores, questions of actual need may arise, and a market analysis (see below) may be performed. Once need has been determined, it is necessary to develop guidelines for designing and building the structure. The first step in this process is to determine how the building is to be used——its overall function and the purposes various spaces within it must serve.③ In a residence, for example, the potential occupant must determine his needs: living, sleeping, food preparation, dining, bathroom, storage areas and special design features, such as a fireplace, wood panelling, and air conditioning. Typically, a residence does not require very comprehensive programming or study. The potential owner or occupant may do nothing more than describe his desires to an architect or builder, who then translates them into design sketches.④

Larger buildings, such as offices, schools, and industrial buildings, require more comprehensive programming. School planners, for example, may attempt to project future student population in order to determine the size of the building. Present and future curricula may be analyzed before a specific design program, including classrooms, gymnasium, library, etc., is drawn up.

In most countries, if a project under development is to be sold or leased, the ability of the owner to market the project at a reasonable return will be critical in determining the project's feasibility. Marketing analysis is undertaken for projects such as multifamily housing, office, commercial, and selected industrial buildings, and even new towns. The method used can be either simple or comprehensive and complex. The approach will vary with the type of construction. In determining the market for a housing project, for example, analysts may examine the supply of housing in the area, projected population and employment, and the levels of income expected by future residents. In this way both the extent and market value of housing demand can be estimated. The extent of market competition is usually also analyzed.

Site Selection and land Acquisition

Before the market analysis can be completed, there must be a decision on the approximate geographic location of the project. To make this decision, specific information is needed. This kind of information is typically obtained and organized in map form. Another important map tool is a diagram showing areas of accessibility to home, to work, or to a shopping centre. In considering a shopping center, for example, the distance of the site from potential shoppers is of major importance. In a project such as a general office building, the distance of the site from major transportation lines is usually a consideration.

As the market analysis progresses, various site advantages and disadvantages can be considered. Finally, one site is given priority over others under consideration.⑤ Final site selection is generally delayed until the financial feasibility study is well underway.⑥

Notes

①必须选好场地，并确定其经济上的可行性。
②当一座建筑物的功能还未能确定之前，人们往往已经决定建造它了。
③本程序的第一步是确定如何使用该建筑物——它的全部功能及内部不同空间要起的作用。
④nothing more than 只不过是。
⑤最后，某一个地点会比其它地点优先考虑。
⑥但一般都推迟到经济的可行性研究全面进行时才能最后选定场地。

Reading Material B

Building

The purpose of a building is to provide a shelter for the performance of human activities. From the time of the cave dwellers to the present, one of the first needs of man has been a shelter from the elements. In a more general sense, the art of building encompasses all of man's efforts to control his environment and direct natural forces to his own needs. ① This art includes, in addition to buildings, all the civil engineering structures such as dams, canals, tunnels and bridges.

The scientific basis for the design of buildings as shelters and for the design of civil engineering structures for other purposes is identical. It is only as a result of the specialized requirements of our modern society that these two fields have developed along separate paths. ②In a similar manner, the master builder concerned with the building as a shelter is no longer an individual; his work is done by a team of several specialists: the planner, the architect, the engineer and the builder. The execution of a modern building depends on the collective talents of this team.

The form of a building is an outgrowth of its function, its environment, and various socioeconomic factors. An apartment building, an office building, and a school differ in form because of the difference in the functions they fulfill. In an apartment building every habitable space, such as living rooms and bedrooms, must have natural light from windows while bathrooms and kitchens can have artificial light and therefore can be in the interior of the building. This set of requirements places a natural limit on the depth of an apartment building. In office buildings, on the other hand, artificial light is accepted for more uniform illumination, and therefore the depth of such buildings is not limited by a need for natural light. ③

Environment may affect both the shape and appearance of a building. An urban school may create its own environment by using blank walls to seal out the city completely, and a country school may develop as an integral part of the landscape, even though both schools fulfill the same function.

Finally, the form of a building is affected by a variety of socioeconomic factors, including land costs, tenancy, building budget, and zoning restrictions. High land costs in urban areas result in high buildings, while low land costs in the country result in low buildings. A housing project for the rich will take a different form than a low-cost housing project. A prestige office building will be more generously budgeted for than other office buildings. The bulk of a building and its outline may be limited by zoning restrictions. In all these examples, buildings with similar functions take on different forms.

Notes

①在更广泛的意义上讲,建筑艺术包含着人类控制环境,利用自然力满足其需要的全部努力。

②只是由于我们现代社会的一些专门需要的结果,这两个领域才沿着各自的道路发展起来。

③相反,在办公楼中,因为需要较均匀的照明,采用人工照明。因此,这类建筑物的深度不因需要天然光而受到限制。

UNIT FOURTEEN

Text   Fundamental Objective of Structural Dynamics Analysis

[1]　The primary purpose of this book is to present methods for analyzing the stresses and deflections developed in any given type of structure when it is subjected to an arbitrary dynamic loading. In one sense, the objective may be considered to be the extension of standard methods of structural analysis, which generally are concerned only with static loading, to permit consideration of dynamic loads as well. In this context, the static-loading condition may be looked upon merely as a special form of dynamic loading. However, in the analysis of linear structures it is convenient to distinguish between the static and the dynamic components of the applied loading, to evaluate the response to each type of loading separately, and then to superpose the two response components to obtain the total effect. ① When treated thus, the static and dynamic methods of analysis are fundamentally different in character. ②

[2]　For the purposes of this presentation the term dynamic may be defined simply as time-varying, thus a dynamic load is any load of which the magnitude, direction, or position varies with time. ③ Similarly, the structural response to a dynamic load, i. e. the resulting deflections and stresses, is also time-varying, or dynamic.

[3]　Two basically different approaches are available for evaluating structural response to dynamic loads: deterministic and nondeterministic. The choice of method to be used in any given case depends upon how the loading is defined. If the time variation of loading is fully known, even though it may be highly oscillatory or irregular in character, it will be referred to herein as a prescribed dynamic loading; and the analysis of the response of any specified structural system to a prescribed dynamic loading is defined as a deterministic analysis. On the other hand, if the time variation is not completely known but can be defined in a statistical sense, the loading is termed a random dynamic loading; a nondeterministic analysis correspondingly is the analysis of response to a random dynamic loading. The principal emphasis in this text is placed on development of methods of deterministic dynamic analysis.

[4]　In general, the structural response to any dynamic loading is expressed basically in terms of the displacements of the structure. Thus a deterministic analysis leads to a displacement-time history corresponding to the prescribed loading history; other aspects of the deterministic structural response, such as stresses, strains, internal forces, etc. , are usually obtained as a secondary phase of the analysis, from the previously established displacement patterns. On the other hand, a nondeterministic analysis provides statistical information about the displacements which result from a statistically defined loading. In this case, the time variation of the displacements is not determined, and other aspects of the response, such as stresses, internal forces, etc. , must

be evaluated directly by independent nondeterministic analysis rather than from the displacement results.

[5]　A structural-dynamic problem differs from its static-loading counterpart in two important respects. The first difference to be noted, by definition, is the time-varying nature of the dynamic problem. Because the load and the response vary with time, it is evident that a dynamic problem does not have a single solution, as a static problem does. Instead the analyst must establish a succession of solutions corresponding to all times of interest in the response history. Thus a dynamic analysis is clearly more complex and time-consuming than a static analysis.

[6]　However, a more fundamental distinction between static and dynamic problems is illustrated in Fig. 14-1(See Reading Material B). If a simple beam is subjected to a static load p, as shown in Fig. 1(a), its internal moments and shears and deflected shape depend directly upon the given load and can be computed from p by established principles of force equilibrium. On the other hand, if the load $p(t)$ is applied dynamically, as shown in Fig. 14-1(b), the resulting displacements of the beam are associated with accelerations which produce inertia forces resisting the accelerations.④ Thus the internal moments and shears in the beam in Fig. 14-1(b) must equilibrate not only the externally applied force but also the inertia forces resulting from the accelerations of the beam.

[7]　Inertia forces which resist accelerations of the structure in this way are the most important distinguishing characteristic of a structural-dynamics problem. In general, if the inertia forces represent a significant portion of the total load equilibrated by the internal elastic forces of the structure, then the dynamic character of the problem must be accounted for in its solution. On the other hand, if the motions are so slow that the inertia forces are negligibly small, the analysis for any desired instant of time may be made by static structural-analysis procedures even though the load and response may be time-varying.

New Words and Expressions

dynamics * [dai'næmiks]	n.	(动)力学
deflection [di'flekʃən]	n.	挠度；偏角
in one sense		从某种意义上讲
in this context		由于这个原因；对此
superpose ['sjuːpə'pəuz]	vt.	叠加
effect [i'fekt]	n.	效应
fundamentally [ˌfʌndə'mentəli]	ad.	根本地
presentation * [ˌprezən'teiʃən]	n.	提出，展示，外观
deterministic * [diˌtəːmi'nistik]	a.	确定的；数定的
oscillatory * [ɔ'sileitəri]	a.	振动的，摆动的
herein ['hiə'in]	ad.	在这里；在本书中

strain[strein]	n.	应变；变形
correspondingly[ˌkɔris'pɔndiŋli]	ad.	相应地
statistically[stə'tistikəli]	ad.	统计(学)地
counterpart['kauntəpɑːt]	n.	对应物；对方
moment['məumənt]	n.	弯矩
dynamically[dai'næmikəli]	ad.	动力地
equilibrate[iːkwi'laibreit]	v.	(使)平衡
externally[eks'təːnəli]	ad.	在外部；在国外
inertia * [i'nəːʃiə]	n.	惯性
inertia force		惯性力
negligibly * ['neglidʒəbli]	ad.	微不足道地，很小地

Notes

① …it is… it 是形式主语，to distinguish…to evaluate…to superpose 三个不定式做主语。

② …when treated… 是一个省略句，实为 when they are treated…。

③ …of which … 是由 prep. ＋ which 组成的定语从句，修饰 any load。

④ …which produce … 是 acceleration, 的定语从句；resisting…为现在分词短语做 inertia forces 的定语。

Exercises

Reading Comprehension

Ⅰ. Choose the most suitable alternative to complete the following sentences.

1. The standard methods of structural analysis are usually related to ＿＿＿＿＿.
    A. static loading
    B. dynamic loading
    C. only static loading but not dynamic loading
    D. Both A and B

2. In the book, much attention has been paid to ＿＿＿＿＿.
    A. prescribed dynamic loading
    B. random dynamic loading
    C. methods of deterministic dynamic analysis
    D. methods of non-deterministic dynamic analysis

3. The deterministic and non-deterministic analyses are two ways to evaluate ＿＿＿＿＿.
    A. the response of any specified structural system
    B. structural response to dynamic loads

C. how to define the loading

   D. how to decide the time variation

4. Why is the dynamic analysis more complex than the static analysis?

   A. A dynamic problem has more than one solution.

   B. The load and the response vary with time.

   C. The analyst must have a number of solutions.

   D. A static problem has only one solution.

5. The most important character of a stractural-dynamics problem is _____.

   A. the inertia force

   B. time-varying

   C. the internal elastic forces

   D. resisting acceleration

II. From the list below choose the most appropriate headings for each of the paragraphs in the text, then put the paragraph numbers in the brackets.

   A. Two kinds of analyses   ( )

   B. The purpose of the book   ( )

   C. The most significant feature   ( )

   D. A more important difference   ( )

   E. The definition of dynamic   ( )

   F. The first difference   ( )

   G. Two methods and how to use them   ( )

III. Complete the following sentences with the information given in the text.

1. In this context, the static-loading condition may _____ as _____.

2. For the purpose of this presentation, the term dynamic may _____ as _____; thus a dynamic load is any load of which _____.

3. In general, the structural response to any dynamic loading _____ in terms of _____.

4. A structural-dynamic problem differs from _____ in _____.

5. If the inertia forces represent _____ of the total load equilibrated by _____, then the dynamic character of the problem must _____ in its solution.

Vocabulary

I. Choose one word or expression which is the most similar in meaning to the word underlined in the given sentence.

1. Most of women buy this kind of soap because of the prettiness of its <u>presentation</u>.

   A. covering   B. coating

   C. complexion   D. appearance

2. But your <u>deterministic</u> beliefs leave no room for my free will.

A. undoubted
B. definite
C. distinctive
D. reliable

3. In Britain the robin is a small bird, but its <u>counterpart</u> in America is much bigger.
   A. partner
   B. equivalent
   C. couple
   D. competitor

4. When he was young, he studied <u>externally</u> for a university degree.
   A. outside
   B. exteriorly
   C. abroad
   D. foreign

5. His contribution to the effort was <u>negligibly</u> small.
   A. slightly
   B. ignorantly
   C. neglectfuly
   D. negligently

II. Match the words in Column A with their corresponding definitions or explanations in Column B.

A

1. deflection
2. dynamics
3. displacement
4. equilibrate
5. inertia

B

a. the force which prevents a thing from being moved when it is stand still and keeps it moving when it is moving
b. to bring into or keep in balance
c. a state of balance
d. a turning aside or off course; deviation
e. the science that deals with matter in movement
f. the act or process of moving from the usual or proper place
g. of or relating to force or power that causes movement
h. an amount being carried out or to be carried

Reading Material A

Organization of the Text

In this development of the theory of structural dynamics, attention will be focused in Part One on the treatment of systems having but a single degree of freedom (SDOF), i.e., systems for which the displacement can be represented by the amplitude of a single coordinate.[①] This class of problem will be studied in detail for two reasons: (1) the behavior of many practical structures can be expressed in terms of a single coordinate, so that the SDOF solution provides an adequate final result; (2) in linear structures of more complex forms, the total response may be expressed as the sum of the responses of a series of SDOF systems. Thus the SDOF analysis technique provides the basis for the vast majority of deterministic structural-dynamic analyses.

Part Two deals with discrete-parameter multi-degree-of-freedom (MDOF) systems, i. e., systems for which the behavior can be expressed in terms of a limited number of coordinates. ② In the analysis of linearly elastic systems, procedures will be presented for evaluating the vibration properties, and then the mode-superposition method will be derived, by means of which the total response is expressed as the sum of the individual responses in the various modes of vibration. The response calculation of each individual mode will be seen to involve a typical SDOF analysis. This superposition procedure is not applicable to nonlinear systems, however, and a step-by-step integration procedure is presented for the solution of such problems.

Dynamic systems having continuously distributed properties will be considered in Part Three. ③ Such systems have an infinite number of degrees of freedom, and their equations of motion are written in the form of partial differential equations. However, it will be shown that the mode-superposition procedure is still applicable and that practical solutions can be obtained even in these cases by considering only a limited number of vibration modes. ④

Parts One to Three are all concerned with deterministic analyses which provide the response history to any given dynamic loading. The probabilistic approach to dynamic analysis is presented in Part Four, starting with the fundamentals of probability theory and including the analysis of both SDOF and MDOF systems.

Often it is not possible to define the excitation of a particular dynamic system fully. In such cases, however, it may be possible to characterize the excitation in a probabilistic manner, which then makes it possible to predict response by probabilistic methods. ⑤ Such results, of course, are just as valuable to the design engineer as those obtained by deterministic means and often more so, particularly when questionable assumptions have been made in order to make a deterministic analysis possible. Certainly one cannot hope, for example, to predict deterministically with any degree of accuracy the future dynamic response of (1) airplanes flying in stormy weather conditions, (2) ships sailing the rough seas, (3) buildings withstanding strong-motion earthquake excitation, (4) missile components subjected to high-noise-level environments, or (5) vehicles traveling over rough roads.

Since probability theory is the basis for nondeterministic analysis, certain fundamentals in this field of study are presented in Chap. 22. These fundamentals are then applied to the characterization of stochastic processes in Chap. 23, which in turn are used to study random vibrations of linear SDOF systems in Chap. 24 and MDOF systems in Chap. 25.

Finally, Part Five deals with applications of structural-dynamics theory to problems of earthquake engineering. It is in such applications that structural-dynamics analysis finds its principal use in civil engineering practice. These basic methods are equally applicable, however, to wind-loading analysis for civil engineering structures or to problems arising in the aerospace industry, in naval architecture, in mechanical engineering, or in any structural system subjected to dynamic loads. ⑥

Notes

① 在论述结构动力学理论方面,在第一篇中将着重处理只具有单自由度的体系(SDOF),这就是可用单个坐标来表达位移的体系。
② 第二篇叙述离散参数多自由度体系(MDOF),也就是说,此种体系的反应可用有限个坐标来表达。
③ 具有连续分布特性的动力体系将在第三篇内讨论。
④ 但是,将会证明,振型叠加法仍然适用,并且即使在这种情况,只考虑有限个振型也能获得实用的解答。
⑤ 但在此种情况下,有可能用概率方式表示扰力的特点,因此也可用概率方法预测体系的反应。
⑥ 这些基本方法同样适用于土木工程结构的风荷载分析,还可用于航天和航天工业、造船、机械工程或任何承受动荷载的结构体系方面所出现的问题。

Reading Material B

Methods of Discretization

In the dynamic system of Fig. 14-1(b), the analysis obviously is greatly complicated by the fact that the inertia forces result from structural displacements which in turn are influenced by the magnitudes of inertia forces.① This closed cycle of cause and effect can be attacked directly only by formulating the problem in terms of differential equations. Furthermore, because the mass of the beam is distributed continuously along its length, the displacements and accelerations must be defined for each point along the axis if the inertia forces are to be completely defined. In this case, the analysis must be formulated in terms of partial differential equations because the position along the span as well as the time must be taken as independent variables.

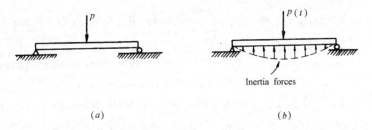

Fig. 14-1 Basic difference between static and dynamic loads:
(a)static loading; (b)dynamic loading.

On the other hand, if the mass of the beam were concentrated in a series of discrete points or lumps, as shown in Fig. 14-2, the analytical problem would be greatly simplified because inertia forces could be developed only at these mass points. In this case it is necessary to define the displacements and accelerations only at these discrete points.

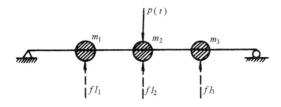

Fig. 14-2 Lumped-mass idealization of a simple beam.

The number of displacement components which must be considered in order to represent the effects of all significant inertia forces of a structure may be termed the number of dynamic degrees of freedom of the structure.[②] For example, if the system of Fig. 14-2 were constrained so that the three mass points could move only in a vertical direction, this would be called a three-degree-of-freedom (3 DOF) system. On the other hand, if these masses were not concentrated in points but had finite rotational inertia, the rotational displacements of the three points would also have to be considered and the system would have 6 DOF. If axial distortions of the beam also were significant, displacements parallel with the beam axis would result and the system would have 9 DOF. More generally, if the structure could deform in three-dimensional space, each mass would have 6 DOF and the system would have 18 DOF. On the other hand, if the masses were concentrated in points so that the rotational inertia might be ignored, the three-dimensional system would then have 9 DOF. On the basis of these considerations, it is clear that a system with continuously distributed mass, as in Fig. 14-1(b), has an infinite number of degrees of freedom.

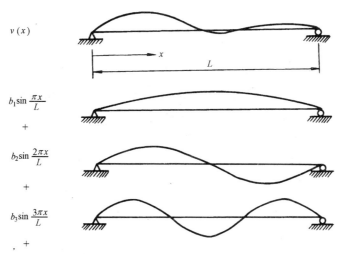

Fig. 14-3 Sine-series representation of simple beam deflection.

The lumped-mass idealization described above provides a simple means of limiting the number of degrees of freedom that must be considered in the analysis of arbitrary problems in structural dynamics.[3] The lumping procedure is most effective in treating systems in which a large proportion of the total mass actually is concentrated in a few discrete points. Then it may be assumed that the mass of the structure which supports these point concentrations can also be included in the lumps and the structure itself considered to be weightless.

In cases where the mass of the system is quite uniformly distributed throughout, however, an alternative approach to limiting the degrees of freedom may be preferable. This procedure is based on the assumption that the deflected shape of the structure can be expressed as the sum of a series of specified displacement patterns; these patterns then become the displacement coordinates of the structure.[4] A simple example of this approach to expressing deflections in structures is the trigonometric-series representation of the deflection of a simple beam. In this case, the deflection may be expressed as the sum of independent sine-wave contributions, as shown in Fig. 14-3, or, in mathematical form,

$$v(x) = \sum_{n=1}^{\infty} b_n \sin \frac{n\pi x}{L}$$

In general, any arbitrary shape compatible with the prescribed support conditions can be represented by an infinite series of such sine-wave components.[5] The amplitudes of the sine-wave shapes may be considered to be the coordinates of the system, and the infinite number of degrees of freedom of the actual beam are represented by the infinite number of terms included in the series. The advantage of this approach is that a good approximation to the actual beam shape can be achieved by a truncated series of sine-wave components; thus a 3 DOF approximation would contain only three terms in the series, etc.

This concept can be further generalized by recognizing that the sine-wave shapes used as the assumed displacement patterns were an arbitrary choice in this example. In general, any shapes $\psi_n(x)$ which are compatible with the prescribed geometric-support conditions and which maintain the necessary continuity of internal displacements may be assumed.[6] Thus a generalized expression for the displacements of any one-dimensional structure might be witten

$$v(x) = \sum_n Z_n \psi_n(x)$$

For any assumed set of displacement functions $\psi_n(x)$, the resulting shape of the structure depends upon the amplitude terms Z_n, which will be referred to as generalized coordinates.[7] The number of assumed shape patterns represents the number of degrees of freedom considered in this form of idealization. In general, better accuracy can be achieved in a dynamic analysis for a given number of degrees of freedom by using the shape-function method of idealization than by the lumped-mass approach. However, it also should be recognized that greater computational effort is required for each degree of freedom when such generalized coordinates are employed.

Notes

①在图 14-1(b) 的动力体系中，由于惯性力由结构位移产生，反过来位移又受惯性力大小的影响，因而分析显得非常复杂。

②为了表示结构全部有意义的惯性力的作用，所必须考虑的位移分量的数目，可称为结构的动力自由度。

③上述集中质量理想化的处理方法提供了一个限制自由度数目的简单方法，而自由度数目在结构动力学的任意问题的分析中都是必须考虑的。

④这个方法是假定结构的挠曲线形状可用一系列规定的位移曲线的和来表达，而这些曲线则成为结构的位移坐标。

⑤一般来说，与所述支承条件相适合的任意形状，都可用无穷多个正弦波分量来表达。

⑥一般来说，任何与所述几何支承条件相适合而且保持内部位移所需连续性的形状 $\psi_n(x)$ 都可被假设。

⑦对于任何假定的一组位移函数 $\psi_n(x)$，所形成的结构形状依赖于幅值项 Z_n，它们都被称为广义坐标。

UNIT FIFTEEN

Text   Contents of Theory of Elasticity

[1]　The theory of elasticity, often called elasticity for short, is the branch of solid mechanics which deals with the stresses and deformations in elastic solids produced by external forces or changes in temperature.

[2]　For students of various engineering disciplines, the purpose of studying elasticity is to analyse the stresses and displacements of structural or machine elements within the elastic range and thereby to check the sufficiency of their strength, stiffness and stability.① Although this purpose is the same as that of studying mechanics of materials and structural mechanics, these three branches of solid mechanics do differ from one another both in the objects studied and in the methods of analysis used.

[3]　Mechanics of materials deals essentially with the stresses and displacements of a structural or machine element in the shape of a bar, straight or curved, which is subjected to tension, compression, shear, bending, or torsion. Structural mechanics, on the basis of mechanics of materials, deals with the stresses and displacements of a structure in the form of a bar system, such as a truss or a rigid frame. As to the structural elements which are not in the form of a bar, such as blocks, plates, shells, dams and foundations, they are analysed only in the theory of elasticity. Moreover, in order to analyse a bar element thoroughly and precisely, it is necessary to apply the theory of elasticity.

[4]　Although bar-shaped elements are studied both in mechanics of materials and in theory of elasticity, the methods of analysis used in the two subjects are not entirely the same. When such an element subjected to external loads is studied in mechanics of materials, some assumptions are usually made on the strain condition or the stress distribution. These assumptions simplify the mathematical derivation to a certain extent, but often inevitably reduce the degree of accuracy of the results obtained. In elasticity, however, the study of a bar-shaped element usually does not need those assumptions. Thus the results obtained are more accurate and may be used to check the approximate results obtained in mechanics of materials.

[5]　For example, when the problem of bending of a straight beam under transverse loads is analysed in mechanics of materials, it is assumed that a plane section of the beam remains plane after bending. This assumption leads to the linear distribution of bending stresses. In the theory of elasticity, however, one can solve the problem without this assumption and prove that if the depth of the beam is not much smaller than the span length, the stress distribution will be far from linear variation, and the maximum tensile stress is seriously undervalued in mechanics of materials.②

[6]　Another example is the calculation of stresses in a prismatical tension member with a hole. It is assumed in mechanics of materials that the tensile stresses are uniformly distributed

across the net section of the member, whereas the precise analysis in the theory of elasticity shows that the stresses are by no means uniform, but are concentrated near the hole; the maximum stress at the edge of the hole is far greater than the average stress across the net section.

[7] Before the twentieth century, bar systems were formally analysed only in structural mechanics and not in elasticity. In spite of this convention, in this century many engineers used a joint application of the two branches of solid mechanics, with the mutual infiltration of the two as a result. The utilization of various methods of analysis in structural mechanics greatly strengthened the theory of elasticity and thus enabled engineers to obtain the solutions of many complicated problems in elasticity. Although these solutions are approximate theoretically, they prove to be scientifically accurate for engineering designs. For example, using the finite element method developed in the last thirty years, we can solve a problem in elasticity by the discretization of the body concerned and then the application of the displacement method, the force method, or the mixed method in structural mechanics.③ This is a brilliant example of the joint application of the two branches of solid mechanics.

[8] Moreover, in the design of a structure, we can utilize the different branches of solid mechanics for different members of the structure, and even for different parts of a single member, to get the most satisfactory results with the least amount of work.④

[9] The students should not pay too much attention to the fuzzy and temporary dividing lines between the three courses in solid mechanics. On the contrary, they are advised to note all the possibilities of joint application of the three courses.

New Words and Expressions

elasticity * [ˌelæˈstisəti]	n.	弹性,伸缩性
torsion * [ˈtɔːʃn]	n.	扭转
truss [trʌs]	n.	构架,桁架
transverse * [trænzˈvəːs]	a.	横向的,横断的
undervalue [ˌʌndəˈvæljuː]	vt.	低估,轻视
prismatical [prizˈmætikl]	a.	等截面的,棱柱的
infiltration [infilˈtreiʃn]	n.	渗透,渗透性
formally [ˈfɔːməli]	ad.	正式地,合乎礼仪地
scientifically [ˌsaiənˈtifikəli]	ad.	科学地
sufficiency [səˈfiʃnsi]	n.	足够的分量,充足
theoretically [ˌθiəˈretikli]	ad.	理论上地
finite * [ˈfainait]	a.	有限的
discretization [disˌkriːtiˈzeiʃn]	n.	离散化
fuzzy [ˈfʌzi]	a.	模糊的

Notes

①两个不定式短语 to analyse … 和 to check … 作系词 is 的并列表语，对 thereby 给以说明。

②句中第一个 and 连接与 solve 并列的谓语动词 prove，第二个 and 连接 prove 所带的并列宾语从句。

③by 词后分别接四个并列的介词宾语，作谓语 can solve a problem 的方式状语。

④不定式短语 to get … 作目的状语。

Exercises

Reading Comprehension

Ⅰ. Choose the most suitable alternative to complete the following sentences.

1. The theory of elasticity is the branch of _____.

   A. structural mechanics

   B. mechanics of materials

   C. solid mechanics

   D. finite element

2. The methods of analysis used in the two subjects are _____.

   A. partly uniform

   B. completely different

   C. not quite equal

   D. not entirely the same

3. These assumptions simplify the _____ to a certain extent.

   A. elastic inference

   B. mathematical derivation

   C. stress distribution

   D. accurate results

4. If the depth of the beam is not much smaller than the span length, the stress distribution will be _____.

   A. far from linear variation

   B. precisely uniform

   C. bar-shaped

   D. from mutual infiltration

5. It is assumed in mechanics of materials that the _____ are uniformly distributed across the net section of the member.

   A. bending stresses

   B. stress distribution

C. tensile stresses

D. average stress

II. From the list below choose the most appropriate headings for each of the paragraphs in the text, then put the paragraph number in the brackets.

A. The purpose of studying elasticity ( )

B. The example of the different methods used in the problem of bending ( )

C. The contents of the theory of elasticity ( )

D. Attention to all the possibilities of joint applications ( )

E. The different methods used in the two branches ( )

F. The significance of the joint application ( )

G. The types of problems dealt with by the three branches ( )

H. Properly using the joint application leading to the best result ( )

I. An example of the different methods used in calculation of stresses ( )

III. Complete the following sentences with the information given in the text.

1. The theory of elasticity deals with the _____ in elastic solids produced by _____ or _____.

2. The structural elements which are not in the form of a bar, such as _____ are analysed only in the theory of elasticity.

3. Thus the results obtained are _____ and may be used _____ obtained in _____.

4. Using the finite element, engineers can solve a problem in elasticity by four methods. They are:

1) _____.

2) _____.

3) _____.

4) _____.

5. We can utilize _____ of solid mechanics for _____ of the structure, and even for _____ of a single member.

Vocabulary

I. Choose one word or expression which is the most similar in meaning to the word underlined in the given sentence.

1. The X—ray showed that he had a (n) <u>deformation</u> of the spine.

   A. abnormal shape   B. change

   C. variation   D. twist

2. Some hotels became hostels after the <u>structural</u> alternations were made to the buildings.

   A. construction   B. partial

   C. foundation   D. framework

3. Relation <u>derivation</u> is often applied in solving mathematical problems.
   A. conclusion   B. deduction
   C. connection   D. agreement
4. These photographs have come out all <u>fuzzy.</u>
   A. indistinct   B. indefinite
   C. confused   D. dim
5. Jim's contribution cannot be <u>undervalued</u> to the research.
   A. undertaken   B. misjudged
   C. underestimated   D. minimized

II. Match the words in Column A with their corresponding definitions or expressions in Column B.

A	B
1. transverse	a. of tension
2. infiltration	b. lying or acting in a crosswise direction
3. torsion	c. framework supporting a roof, building, etc.
4. discretization	d. displacing or being displaced
5. truss	e. the state of separation
	f. twisting, esp of one end of something while the other end is held fixed
	g. the act of infiltrating
	h. rate at too low a value, underestimate

Reading Material A

Basic Assumptions in Classical Elasticity

To evaluate the stresses, strains and displacements in an elasticity problem, we must derive a series of basic equations and boundary conditions. During the process of derivation, however, if we consider all the influential factors in an all-round way, the results obtained will be so complicated that practically no solutions can be found. Therefore, we have to make some basic assumptions about the properties of the body considered and on the range of our study.① Under such assumptions, we can neglect some of the influential factors of minor importance temporarily, thus simplifying the basic equations and the boundary conditions.② In this text, we will comply with the following assumptions in classical elasticity:

(1) The body is continuous, i.e., the whole volume of the body is filled with continuous matter, without any void. Only under this assumption, can the physical quantities in the body, such as stresses, strains and displacements, be continuously distributed and thereby expressed by continuous functions of coordinates in space. In reality, all engineering materials are

composed of elementary particles and do not accord with the assumption of continuity. However, it may be conceived that this assumption will lead to no significant errors so long as the dimensions of the body are very large in comparison with those of the particles and with the distances between neighboring particles.

(2) The body is perfectly elastic, i.e., it wholly obeys Hooke's law of elasticity, which shows the linear relations between the stress components and the strain components. Under this assumption, the elastic constants will be independent of the magnitudes of these components. The justification for this assumption lies in the physical behavior of nearly all materials in engineering construction.

(3) The body is homogeneous so that the elastic properties are the same throughout the body. Thus, the elastic constants will be independent of the location in the body. Under this assumption, we may analyse an elementary volume isolated from the body and then apply the results of analysis to the entire body.

(4) The body is isotropic so that the elastic properties are the same in all directions. Thus, the elastic constants will be independent of the orientation of coordinate axes.

Most engineering materials do not satisfy the above two assumptions completely. Structural steel, for instance, when studied with a microscope, is seen to consist of crystals of various kinds and various orientations. It seems that the material is far from being homogeneous and isotropic. However, since the dimensions of any single crystal are very small in comparison with those of the entire body, and since the crystals are orientated at random, the behavior of a piece of steel, on average, appears to justify the assumptions of homogeneity and isotropy. This is the reason why the solutions in elasticity based on these assumptions can be applied to steel structures with very great accuracy so long as none of the members has been subjected to the process of rolling which may produce a definite orientation of the crystals. In contrast with steel, wood is definitely not isotropic, since the elastic properties of wood in the direction of the grain differ greatly from those in the perpendicular directions. In assuming isotropic material, we shall of course exclude the treatment of wooden structures.

(5) The displacements and strains are small, i.e., the displacement components of all points of the body during deformation are very small in comparison with its original dimensions, and the strain components and the rotations of all line elements are much smaller than unity. Thus, when we formulate the equilibrium equations relevant to the deformed state, we may use the lengths and angles of the body before deformation. ③In addition, when we formulate the geometrical equations involving strains and displacements, we may neglect the squares and products of the small quantities. ④ These two measures are necessary to linearize the algebraic and differential equations in elasticity for their easier solution.

Notes

① 因此,我们必须作出有关所研究物体及我们研究范围的一些基本假设。
② 在这样的假设下,可暂时忽略一些不重要的影响因素,从而简化基本方程式和边界条件。
③ 当我们建立与变形状态相关的平衡方程式时,可采用物体变形前的长度和角度。
④ 此外,当我们建立关于应变和位移的几何方程时,可忽略微小数量的平方和乘积。

Reading Material B

Members in a State of Two-Dimensional Stress

Within the scope of the formulas developed in this text, bodies in a state of two-dimensional stress can be studied as was done in the preceding example.① A great many points in a stressed body may be investigated for the magnitude and direction of the principal stresses. Then, to study the general behavior of the stresses, selected points can be interconnected to give a visual interpretation of the various aspects of the computed data. For example, the points of algebraically equal principal stresses, regardless of their sense, when connected, provide a "map" of stress contours.② Any point lying on a stress contour has a principal stress of the same algebraic magnitude.

Similarly, the points at which the directions of the minimum principal stresses form a constant angle with the x-axis can be connected. Moreover, since the principal stresses are mutually perpendicular, the direction of the maximum principal stresses through the same points also forms a constant angle with the x-axis. The line so connected is a locus of points along which the principal stresses have parallel directions. This line is called an isoclinic line. The adjective isoclinic is derived from two Greek words, isos meaning equal and klino meaning slope or incline. Three isoclinic lines can be found by inspection in a rectangular prismatic beam subjected to transverse load acting normal to its axis.③ The lines corresponding to the upper and lower boundaries of a beam form two isoclinic lines as, at the boundary, the flexural stresses are the principal stresses and act parallel to the boundaries.④ On the other hand, the flexural stress is zero at the neutral axis, and only there do pure shearing stresses exist. These pure shearing stresses transform into principal stresses, all of which act at an angle of 45° with the axis of the beam. Hence, another isoclinic line (the 45° isoclinic) is located on the axis of the beam. The other isoclinic lines are curved and are more difficult to determine.

Another set of curves can be drawn for a stressed body for which the magnitude and the sense of the principal stresses are known at a great many points. A curve whose tangent is changing in direction to conform with the direction of the principal stresses is called a principal stress trajectory or isostatic line. Like the isoclinic lines, the principal stress trajectories do not connect the points of equal stresses, but rather indicate the directions of the principal stresses. Since the principal stresses at any point are mutually perpendicular, the principal stress trajectories for the two principal stresses form a family of orthogonal (mutually perpendicular) curves.

Notes

①在本课涉及的方程式范围内,以二维应力形态出现的物体就象在上一个例子里出现过一样可以进行研究。

②例如,主应力代数值相等的那些点,不管它们意义如何,当被连接在一起时会形成一个应力轮廓图。

③在承受垂直于梁轴的横向荷载的矩形截面梁中可观察到三条等倾线。

④在梁的上下边界形成两条等倾线,因为弯应力为主要应力,与边界平行。

UNIT SIXTEEN

Text　Historical Development of Finite Element Method

[1]　The term 'finite element' appears to have been coined by Clough in an article published in 1960. It was used to describe a computational approach to the analysis of elastic membranes in which the continuum was divided into a discrete number of small but finite subregions or 'elements'. The idea itself was not new. In fact, the notion of dividing a continuum into finite pieces had been suggested by Courant in 1949. The practical implementation of such an approach only materialized in the mid—1950s, however, with the advent of digital computation. It was Turner, Clough and others who then combined the idea of discrete elements with the 'stiffness' approach to matrix structural analysis, to produce a systematic procedure which later became known as the finite element method. ① An interesting account of these early developments is to be found in Clough's own commentary on the period.

[2]　The popularity of the method grew rapidly in the years that followed. Within ten years of the invention of the term, more than one thousand articles dealing with finite elements had been published in the scientific literature. Two decades later, the number of articles listed in the COMPENDEX-PLUS engineering index approaches 50,000. This phenomenal rate of growth is a reflection of the degree to which the finite element concept has complemented the emerging capabilities of the digital computer. Most importantly, it has lent itself to the development of multipurpose programs. In the late sixties, this gave rise to the first, commercial, finite element computer codes. These were programs, capable of solving different physical problems through changes to the input data rather than to the code itself. ② Such programs have expanded and proliferated in the years since and now include such industry standards as NASTRAN, ABAQUS, ADINA, ANSYS, PAFEC, SAP, MARC and EASE, to name but a few. More recently they have been joined by a new generation of PC or workstation orientated codes such as MSC/PAL, ANSYS-PC, SAP90, COSMOS/M, ALGOR and so on. Their application to practical problems of stress analysis constitutes one of the major advances in mechanical and structural design of the present era.

[3]　Also contributing to the rapid growth of the method from the late sixties onwards was the realization that it could be applied to problems other than those of solid and structural analysis. The first suggestion that this might be the case came with the work of Zienkiewicz and others in demonstrating that the method could be used for field problems involving Laplace's and Poisson's equations (steady state thermal conduction, for example, or potential flow of an inviscid fluid). These developments were accompanied by the realization, also in the early sixties, that the Galerkin approach and others 'weighted residuals' techniques could be used as a theoretical basis for applying finite elements to virtually any problem which could be expressed in terms of partial differential equations. ③ As a consequence, current areas of application now

include fluid mechanics, aerodynamics, acoustics, lubrication theory, geomechanics, atmospheric dynamics, electromagnetic theory and so on.

[4]   Confining our discussion now to solid and structural applications, the finite element method was well advanced by the late sixties in its capacity to solve practical two and three-dimensional problems in linear elasticity. However, it still required substantial computation —— in the context of that commonly available at the time —— and was accessible only to those engaged in large-scale industrial or institutional research. ④ One of the most significant recent developments in the application of the method has arisen not so much from any specific advance in the methodology itself (new element formulations, solution algorithms etc.) but simply from the steady decrease in the effective cost of computing. This has brought finite element computation within the mainstream of engineering practice by making it accessible, for routine design analysis, to engineers with relatively modest computational facilities at their disposal. ⑤ Many commercial programs now operate effectively on engineering workstations or personal computers and performs substantial analyses for a small fraction of the cost associated with such calculations a decade or so ago. This is clearly a trend which has a long way to run and one which will make the method even more accessible to the engineering profession in years to come.

[5]   A side effect of the same phenomenon, the inexorable decrease in the real cost, of computing, has been the use of computer graphics in the engineering environment. This in turn has driven the growth in computer aided design and manufacture (CAD/CAM). Practical implementation of the element method has been encouraged by such developments since the generation of finite element models can readily be integrated with the geometric modelling techniques which lie at the heart of the CAD/CAM revolution. There are consequently few CAD systems today which do not provide a facility for the interchange of geometrical information with compatible finite element programs. This integration between geometric design (using a CAD system) and quantitative analysis (using a finite element code) has rendered the preparation of finite element data and the display of the results of finite element analysis, if not trivial, at least an order of magnitude less time consuming than was the case with the finite element programs of the sixties and seventies. ⑥

New Words and Expressions

computational * [ˌkɔmpjuːˈteiʃənl]	a.	计算的
membrane * [ˈmembrein]	n.	薄膜
continuum [kənˈtinjuəm]	n.	连续体
discrete * [disˈkriːt]	a.	离散的，分立的
algorithm [ˈælgəriðəm]	n.	计算，算法
institutional [ˌinstiˈtjuːʃənl]	a.	惯例的，慈善机构的
inviscid [inˈvisid]	a.	非粘滞性的

multipurpose['mʌlti'pə:pəs]	a.	多方面的
onwards['ɔnwədz]	ad.	向前地
subregion['sʌbˌri:dʒən]	n.	子结构,子域
notion * ['nəuʃən]	n.	概念,观念
implementation * [ˌimplimen'teiʃən]	v.	执行,落实
advent * ['ædvənt]	n.	出现,到来
commentary['kɔməntəri]	n.	评论,纪事
popularity * [ˌpɔpju'læriti]	n.	普及,流行
phenomenal[fi'nɔminl]	a.	现象的
complement * [ˌkɔmpli'ment]	vt.	补充,补足
proliferate[prəu'lifəreit]	vt.	增生,扩散
orient * ['ɔ:rient]	vt.	定位
residual * [re'zidjuəl]	n.	剩余
differential * [difə'renʃəl]	a.	微分的
aerodynamics[ˌɛərəudai'næmiks]	n.	空气动力学
acoustics[ə'ku:stiks]	n.	声学
lubrication * [ˌlu:bri'keiʃən]	n.	润滑
geomechanics[ˌdʒiəumi'kæniks]	n.	地球力学,地质力学
electromagnetic * [iˌlektrəumæg'netik]	a.	电磁的
accessible[ək'sesəbl]	a.	易接近的
methodology * [ˌmeθə'dɔlədʒi]	n.	方法论
mainstream['meinˌstri:m]	n.	主系统,主流
inexorable[in'eksərəbl]	a.	残酷无情的
graphics * ['græfiks]	n.	绘图学,制图学
integrate * ['intigreit]	vt.	使成整体,使合成
compatible * [kəm'pætəbl]	a.	兼容的
quantitative * ['kwɔntitətiv]	a.	定量的
trivial * ['triviəl]	a.	无足轻重的
interchange * [ˌintə'tʃeindʒ]	vt.	交换,调换
workstation['wə:k'steiʃn]	n.	工作站

Notes

①介词短语 to matrix structural analysis 作名词 approach 的定语。不定式 to produce⋯ method 作目的状语。

②capable of 为形容词短语作 programs 的非限定性定语,介词短语 to the input data 和 to the code itself 为 changes 的定语。

③that the Galerkin approach 作 realization 的同位语从句,which could be expressed 作 problem 的定语从句。

④介词短语 in the context of that…time 为插入语，起条件状语作用，其中的 that 指 computation，形容词 available 作 that 的后置定语，and was accessible to …research 作 required 的并列谓语。

⑤句中 it 指 computation，accessible 作 it 的宾语补足语，at their disposal 为介词短语作 facilities 的定语，意为"手边的"或"运用自如的"。

⑥if 从句省略了主语 the display of the results of finite element analysis 和系词 are；名词短语 at least an order… seventies 作宾语补足语；less time consuming… seventies 作 order 的定语。

Exercises

Reading Comprehension

Ⅰ. Choose the most suitable alternative to complete the following sentences.

1. In fact, the notion of dividing _____ had been suggested by Courant in 1943.

    A. a subregion into digital numbers

    B. a continuum into elastic membranes

    C. a continuum into finite pieces

    D. a field problem into discrete elements

2. In the late sixties, this _____ the first, commercial, finite element computer codes.

    A. brought about the appearance of

    B. raised the position of

    C. promoted the changes to

    D. proliferated the developments of

3. It was Turner, Clough and others who then combined _____ with the _____ to matrix structural analysis.

    A. the notion of finite elements; stiffness approach

    B. the idea of digital computation; Galerkin approach

    C. the concept of weighted residuals; computational approach

    D. the idea of discrete elements; stiffness approach

4. One of the most significant recent developments in the application of the method has risen from _____.

    A. any specific advance in the methodology itself

    B. the steady decrease in the effective cost of computing

    C. the application within the mainstream of engineering practice

    D. the utilization of the relative modest computational facilities

5. There are consequently few CAD systems today which _____ for the interchange of

geometrical information with compatible finite element programs.

A. have provided a program
B. don't offer a computation
C. must render a feature
D. do not provide a facility

II. From the list below choose the most appropriate headings for each of the paragraphs in the text, then put the paragraph numbers in the brackets.

A. The realization of the practical method and the fields concerning the application of it ( )
B. The appearance of the finite element method ( )
C. The combination of CAD/CAM with the finite element method ( )
D. The growing popularity of the finite element method ( )
E. The advanced feature of the finite element method and its future trend ( )

III. Complete the following sentences with the information given in the text.

1. The term finite element was used to describe _____ to the analysis of _____.

2. The combination of the idea of _____ with the _____ to matrix structural analysis produced a systematic procedure known as the _____.

3. Galerkin approach and other weighted residuals techniques could be used as _____ for applying _____ to virtually any problem which could be expressed in terms of _____.

4. Current areas of application now include:
    1)_____   2)_____
    3)_____   4)_____
    5)_____   6)_____
    7)_____

5. The generation of _____ can readily be integrated with _____.

Vocabulary

I. Choose one word or expression which is the most similar in meaning to the word underlined in the given sentence.

1. All at the meeting were tired of the chairman as he talked of a series of <u>discrete</u> events in his speech.
    A. connected   B. irrelative
    C. irrelevant   D. continuous

2. The archives museum keeps documents not <u>accessible</u> to the public.
    A. available   B. useful
    C. forbidden   D. valuable

3. With the <u>advent</u> of the new president, the company began to prosper.
    A. adventure   B. advantage

    C. popularity   D. arrival

4. He is involved in a research oriented medical establishment.

    A. confronting   B. faced with

    C. favouring   D. aimed at

5. The new developments are well integrated with the landscape.

    A. related   B. associated

    C. blended   D. constructed

II. Match the words in Column A with their corresponding definitions or expressions in Column B.

A	B
1. complement	a. scientific study of sound
2. acoustics	b. that can be reached or used
3. trivial	c. to make something complete
4. compatible	d. showing or depending on a difference
5. proliferate	e. that has little importance
	f. that can exist or work in agreement together or with another
	g. increase rapidly in numbers
	h. thing whose structure is continuous not discrete

Reading Material A

General Description of the Finite Element Method

    In the finite element method, the actual continuum or body of matter like solid, liquid or gas is represented as an assemblage of subdivisions called finite elements. These elements are considered to be interconnected at specified joints which are called nodes or nodal points. The nodes usually lie on the element boundaries where adjacent elements are considered to be connected. Since the actual variation of the field variable (like displacement, stress, temperature, pressure or velocity) inside the continuum is not known, we assume that the variation of the field variable inside a finite element can be approximated by a simple function.① These approximating functions (also called interpolation models) are defined in terms of the values of the field variables at the nodes. When field equations (like equilibrium equations) for the whole continuum are written, the new unknowns will be the nodal values of the field variable. By solving the field equations, which are generally in the form of matrix equations, the nodal values of the field variable will be known. Once these are known, the approximating functions define the field variable throughout the assemblage of elements.

    The solution of a general continuum problem by the finite element method always follows an orderly step-by-step process. With reference to static structural problems, the step-by-step procedure can be stated as follows:

Step (i): Discretization of the structure

The first step in the finite element method is to divide the structure or solution region into subdivisions or elements. Hence the structure that is being analyzed has to be modeled with suitable finite elements. The number, type, size and arrangement of the elements have to be decided.

Step (ii): Selection of a proper interpolation or displacement model

Since the displacement solution of a complex structure under any specified load conditions cannot be predicted exactly, we assume some suitable solution within an element to approximate the unknown solution.② The assumed solution must be simple from computational point of view, but it should satisfy certain convergence requirements. In general, the solution or the interpolation model is taken in the form of a polynomial.

Step (iii): Derivation of element stiffness matrices and load vectors

From the assumed displacement model, the stiffness matrix $[K^{(e)}]$ and the load vector $\vec{P}^{(e)}$, of element "e" are to be derived by using either equilibrium conditions or a suitable variational principle.

Step (iv): Assemblage of element equations to obtain the overall equilibrium equations

Since the structure is composed of several finite elements, the individual element stiffness matrices and load vectors are to be assembled in a suitable manner and the overall equilibrium equations have to be formulated as

$$[K]\vec{\Phi} = \vec{P}$$

where $[K]$ is called the assembled stiffness matrix, $\vec{\Phi}$ is the vector of nodal displacements and $\vec{P}$ is the vector of nodal forces for the complete structure.③

Step (v): Solution for the unknown nodal displacements

The overall equilibrium equations have to be modified to account for the boundary conditions of the problem. After the incorporation of the boundary conditions, the equilibrium equations can be expressed as

$$[K]\vec{\Phi} = \vec{P}$$

For linear problems, the vector $\vec{\Phi}$ can be solved very easily. But for nonlinear problems, the solution has to be obtained in a sequence of steps, each step involving the modification of the stiffness matrix $[K]$ and/or the load vector $\vec{P}$.

Step (vi): Computation of element strains and stresses

From the known nodal displacements $\vec{\Phi}$, if required, the element strains and stresses can be computed by using the necessary equations of solid or structural mechanics.④

The terminology used in the above six steps has to be modified if we want to extend the concept to other fields. For example, we have to use the term continuum or domain in place of structure, field variable in place of displacement, characteristic matrix in place of stiffness matrix, and element resultants in place of element strains.

Notes

① 由于连续体内场变量的实际变化（如位移、应力、温度、压力或速度）是一个未知数，我们设定一个有限元内的场变量的实际变化可以用简单的函数来近似。

② 由于在任何特定的载荷条件下，一个复杂结构的位移解不能够被精确地预测出来，我们采用有限元内某一适当的解去近似这个未知的位移解。

③ 因为结构由若干有限元组成，每一有限元的刚度矩阵和荷载向量会以适当的方式集合，与此同时总平衡公式形成：

$$[K]\vec{\Phi} = \vec{P}$$

式中的 $[K]$ 代表集合刚度矩阵，$\vec{\Phi}$ 是位移结点向量，$\vec{P}$ 是整个结构结点力向量。

④ 如果需要，根据已知的结点位移并运用固体力学或结构力学中必要的方程式可计算出有限元的应变与应力。

Reading Material B

Introduction of Displacement Approach

In many phases of engineering the solution of stress and strain distributions in elastic continua is required. Special cases of such problems may range from two—dimensional plane stress or strain distributions, axi-symmetrical solids, plate bending, and shells, to fully three—dimensional solids. In all cases the number of interconnections between any 'finite element' isolated by some imaginary boundaries and the neighbouring elements is infinite. ① It is therefore difficult to see at first glance how such problems may be discretized. The difficulty can be overcome (and the approximation made) in the following manner:

(a) The continuum is separated by imaginary lines or surfaces into a number of 'finite elements'.

(b) The elements are assumed to be interconnected at a discrete number of nodal points situated on their boundaries. ② The displacements of these nodal points will be the basic unknown parameters of the problem, just as in the simple, discrete, structural analysis. ③

(c) A set of functions is chosen to define uniquely the state of displacement within each 'finite element' in terms of its nodal displacements.

(d) The displacement functions now define uniquely the state of strain within an element in terms of the nodal displacements. These strains, together with any initial strains and the constitutive properties of the material will define the state of stress throughout the element and, hence, also on its boundaries.

(e) A system of forces concentrated at the nodes and equilibrating the boundary stresses and any distributed loads is determined, resulting in a stiffness relationship of the form of Eq.④

Once this stage has been reached the solution procedure can follow the standard discrete system pattern described earlier.

Clearly a series of approximations has been introduced. Firstly, it is not always easy to ensure that the chosen displacement functions will satisfy the requirement of displacement continuity between adjacent elements. Thus, the compatibility condition on such lines may be violated (though within each element it is obviously satisfied due to uniqueness of displacements implied in their continuous representation). Secondly, by concentrating the equivalent forces at the nodes, equilibrium conditions are satisfied in the overall sense only. Local violation of equilibrium conditions within each element and on its boundaries will usually arise. The choice of element shape and of the form of the displacement function for specific cases leaves much choice to ingenuity and skill of the engineer, and obviously the degree of approximation which can be achieved will much depend on these factors. The approach outlined here is known as the displacement formulation. So far, the process described is justified only intuitively, but what in fact has been suggested is equivalent to the minimization of the total potential energy of the system in terms of a prescribed displacement field.⑤ If this displacement field is defined in a suitable way, then convergence to the correct result must occur. The process is then equivalent to the well-known Ritz procedure. The recognition of the equivalence of the finite element method with a minimization process was late. However, Courant in 1943 and Prager and Synge in 1947 proposed methods in essence identical. This broader basis of the finite element method allows it to be extended to other continuum problems where a variational formulation is possible. Indeed, general procedures are now available for a finite element discretization of any problem defined by a properly constituted set of differential equations.⑥

Notes

①任何情况下，从设想边界分离出来的任何有限元和相邻单元之间相互连接点数目是无限的。

②这些有限元假定是在位于其边界上的若干个离散的结点处相互连接的。

③正如简单的、离散的结构分析，这些结点位移将是问题的基本未知参数。

④集中在结点并与边界应力及分布荷载相平衡的力系被确定之后，即可形成方程式那样的刚度关系。

⑤到目前为止，上述求解方法只是直观地被认为有道理，但建议的方法事实上等同于按照规定的位移场将体系的全部位能化为最小。

⑥如果用合适的微分方程组求解任何有限元离散法问题，此文涉及的总体步骤是切实可行的。

Appendix I　　Vocabulary

accessible * a. 易接近的		16
acoustics n. 声学		16
adequacy * n 适当		08
adjacent * a. 相邻的		01
admixture n. 添加剂,掺和剂		09
advent * n. 出现,到来		16
aerodynamic a. 空气动力学的		03
aerodynamics n. 空气动力学		16
aggregate * n. 骨料		07
algorithm n. 计算		16
allude vt. 提及(to),提到		10
alternately ad. 另一方面,轮流地		03
alternative n. 取舍		05
ambient * a. 周围的		07
analogous * a. 类似的		01
analogy * n. 相似,类推		11
appreciable * a. 可估计的,可看到的		02
approximation * n. 近似,近似值		06
asbestos * n. 石棉		13
asbestos-cement 石棉水泥板		13
assemblage n. 集合,组装		05
axially ad. 轴向的		01
batch * n. 一批投料量		10
batter n. (做糕饼时用面粉、鸡蛋等调制成的)糊状物		11
Belgium n. 比利时(欧洲国家)		09
blend n. 混合,融合		01
booklet n. 小册子		07
bouncy a. 有弹性的		05
brace n.,v. 支柱;支住		07
bricklayer n. 泥(瓦)工		11
brickmason n. 泥瓦匠		09
brittle * a. 脆性的		02
buckling * n. 屈曲		03

caisson n. 沉箱		12
capability n. 性质,能力		09
cementitious a. (有)粘结性的		11
centroid n. 矩心,形心		01
ceramics n. 陶瓷制品		02
circulation * n. 流线循环,流通		05
clad * v. 在…包上另一层,覆盖		13
cladding n. 包层		13
client * n. 委托人,顾客		13
clinker n. (水泥)熟料;渣块,炉渣		09
cohesive a. 粘结的,粘性的;内聚的		11
colourless a. 无色的		13
column spacing 柱间距		13
combinational a. 结合的,配合的		12
commentary n. 评论,纪事		16
compatible * a. 兼容的		16
competitive * a. 竞争的		05
complement * n. 补充,补足		16
composite a. 合成的		03
compressive a. 压力的,压缩的		01
computational * a. 计算的		16
condensation * n. 冷凝,凝结		13
configuration * n. 构件,构造,形状		03
conglomerate n. 砾岩,石材		07
conical a. 圆锥形的		08
consistency * n. 稠度,浓度		11
constituent * n. 成分,要素		07
contemplate v. 思考,打算		06
context * n. 上下文,情况		12
continuum * n. 连续体		16
contractor * n. 承包人		08
contradistinction n. 对比		03
convergence * n. 收敛性		06
coordinate n. 坐标系,一致		04

141

coordination *	n. 配合,协调	12
correspondingly	ad. 相应地	14
corrosive *	a. 腐蚀性的	08
corrugate	v. 成波状,加工成波纹状	13
counterpart	n. 对应物,对方	14
cross-section	n. 横截面	02
cu ft=cubic foot	立方英尺	10
cure *	vt. 养护(混凝土)	10
curriculum	n. 课程	03
curvilinear	a. 曲线的	07
dampness	n. 潮湿	13
deadening of sound	消声	13
decipher	vt. 解释,注解	12
decompose *	v. 分解	06
deficiency *	n. 缺乏	07
deflect *	v. (使)偏斜,偏转,(使)弯曲	03
deflection	n. 挠度,偏角	14
deform *	v.(使)变形	04
deformable	a. 可变形的	01
deliberate	a. 深思熟虑的	05
denote *	v. 指示,表示	01
derivation *	n. 推导	01
determinant	n. 决定因素,决定物	10
determination	n. 确定,定义	04
deterministic *	a. 确定的,定数的	14
diagrammatic	a. 图解的	03
differential	a. 微分的	16
differentiate *	v. 区别,区分	05
diminish *	v. 减少,缩减	02
discrete *	a. 离散的,分立的	16
discretization	n. 离散化	15
displacement *	n. 位移,转移	04
dividend	n. 利息,股息	03
dome	n. 圆屋顶	05
dominant *	a. 支配的	05
ductile *	a. 可塑的,延性的	02
durability *	n. 耐久性,持久性	10
dwelling	n. 住处,寓所	08
dynamic	a. 动力(学)的	06
dynamically	ad. 动力地	14
dynamics *	n. (动)力学	14
effect	n. 效应	14
elasticity *	n. 弹性,伸缩性	15
electromagnetic *	a. 电磁的	16
eliminate	v. 除去,删去	04
elongate *	v. 伸长,拉长	02
elongation	n. 伸长,拉长	01
emancipate	v. 使不受...束缚	05
embed *	vt. 把...嵌入,放入	10
empirical *	a. 经验的	03
enact	v. 制定	08
ensue	vi. 接着发生,接着而来	09
entity	n. 实体,统一体	08
Eq.	n. 方程(式)	01
equilibrate	vt. (使)平衡	14
equilibrium *	n. 平衡	01
erection	n. 装配	05
erosive	a. 腐蚀(性)的	11
erratic *	a. 不稳的,多变的	09
essence *	n. 本质,实质	07
excess	a. 超量的	07
exemplify *	vt. 举例说明	12
expenditure *	n. 消耗	03
externally	ad. 在外部;在国外	14
fabricate *	v. 制作	03
fabrication	n. 制作	05
facade	n. 正面,表面	12
fascinate *	v. 迷住,强烈吸引	01
feasibility *	n. 可行性	03
finite *	a. 有限的	15
fixture *	n. (房屋的)固定装置	08
folly	n. 蠢事	09
formally	ad. 正式地,合乎礼仪地	15
formulation *	n. 表达,表述	04
fracture *	n. 断裂	02

fundamentally	ad. 根本地		14
fuzzy	a. 模糊的		15
gal=gallon	n. 加仑		10
geology	n. 地质学		12
geomechanics	n. 地球力学,地质力学		16
girder	n. 梁,桁架		06
give	n. 弹性		11
graphics *	n. 绘图学,制图学		16
gravel	n. 砾石,砂砾		10
gypsum	n. 石膏		09
herein	ad. 在这里;在本书中		14
hull *	n. 外壳		03
humanitarian	a. 人道主义的		08
hydrate	vt. 使水合		10
hydration	n. 水化(作用)		07
hydraulic *	a. 水硬的,水力的		09
hydrostatic *	a. 静力学的		01
idealize *	v. 使理想化		06
impervious	a. 不可渗透的,不透过的		10
implementation *	n. 执行,落实		16
impose	v. 把…强加给		08
impulse *	n. 冲动,推动		08
in one sense	从某种意义上讲		14
in this context	由于这个原因;对此		14
incongruously	ad. 不调和地,不一致地		08
inconsistency	n. 不一致性,不相容(性)		04
incorporate *	v. 合并,纳入		06
indelible	a. 不可磨灭的		03
indeterminacy	n. 不确定,不明确		04
indeterminate *	a. 不确定的		04
inertia *	n. 惯性		14
inertia force	惯性力		14
inexorable	a. 残酷无情的		16
infiltration	n. 渗透,渗透性		15
inflating	a. 膨胀的,抬高的		12
ingredient *	n. 成分		07
inherent	a. 内在的,固有的		05
inspection	n. 检查		07
institutional	a. 惯例的		16
insulate *	vt. 使…绝缘		13
insulation	n. 绝缘(层)		13
insulator	n. 绝缘体		13
integrate *	v. 使成整体,结合		05
integrity	n. 完整,完全		05
interchange *	vt. 交换,调换		16
interspatial	a. 空间的		12
inviscid	a. 非粘滞性的		16
irrational	a. 无理的		05
jagged	a. 锯齿状的,参差不齐的		11
jerry	a. 偷工减料的		08
jurisdiction	n. 管辖权,权限		08
kiln	n. 窑		09
kinematic *	a. 运动的,动力学的		04
kips	n. 千磅		01
lateral *	a. 侧面的		02
leeway	n. 可允许的误差		08
lighthouse	n. 灯塔		09
limestone	n. 石灰石		09
linear *	a. 直线的		02
lubrication	n. 润滑		16
magnitude *	n. 大小,尺寸		01
mainstream	n. 主系统,主流		16
markedly *	ad. 显著地		07
masonry	n. 砖石建筑		09
masonry unit	砌块		11
mass	n. 块		10
membrane *	n. 薄膜		16
metallic *	a. 金属的		02
metallurgist	n. 冶金学家		03
methodology *	n. 方法论		16
migrate *	vi. 迁移,流动,移动		10
minimize *	v. 使减少到最少,使…降到最低		12
misalignment	n. 误差,未校准		03
mislocated	a. 放错位置的		07
moldable	a. 可塑的		07

143

moment n. 弯矩	14	透水的	10
monitor n. 采光顶,天窗	13	postulate * v. 公理	03
monolithic * a. 整体的	07	pozzolan n. 一种混合水泥(波特兰	
mortar n. 水泥,灰浆	09	水泥与火山灰的混合物)	09
mullion n. (窗的)直棂	05	precast v. 浇铸,预制	07
multi-storey .n. 多层	13	precedent n. 先例	03
multipurpose a. 多方面的	16	preconceived a. 事先想好的	12
multitude * n. 许多,大批	11	prediction n. 预测,预言	06
municipality n. 市,市政	08	prefabricated a. 预制的	12
negligibly * ad. 微不足道地,很小地	14	presentation * n. 提出,展示;外观	14
nondimensional a. 无量纲的	01	prestrain n. 预(加)应变,预加载	04
nonlinear a. 非线性的	02	prevail v. 战胜,占优势	06
notion * n. 概念,观念	16	prismatic a. 等截面的	01
obsolete * a. 已不用的,已废弃的	10	prismatical a. 等截面的,棱柱的	15
obviate v. 消除,避免	05	proliferate vt. 增生,扩散	16
occupant n. 居住者,占用者	05	pyramid n. 金字塔	09
offset * vt. 抵消,补偿	12	quantitative * a. 定量的	16
onwards ad. 向前地	16	quarry vt. 采石,采沙	09
ordinate n. 纵坐标	02	quicklime n. 生石灰	09
orient vt. 定位	16	ram vt. 夯实	09
oscillatory * a. 振动的,摆动的	14	ramification n. 分枝,细节	12
pancake n. 薄煎饼	11	random * a. 随机的	06
patent * n. 专利权,专利证	09	rational a. 合理的	03
pavement n. 铺建过的路面	09	realistic * a. 现实的	01
perch v. 放置…于高处	08	recessive a. 后退的	05
phase n. 方法,步骤	03	redundant a. 多余的,过剩的	04
phenomenal a. 现象的	16	rental a. 租用的	12
placement * n. 浇筑,灌筑	07	residual * n. 剩余	16
planar * a. 平面的,平的	06	resultant * n. 合力	01
plaster a. 墁灰,灰泥	03	rigidity * n. 刚性,刚度	07
plasticity * n. 可塑性,成形性	06	rigorous * a. 严格的,严厉的	06
plot v. 测定,标绘	02	rotary a. 旋转的	09
plumb n. 管子	08	rupture * n. 裂开	05
plywood n. 胶合板	13	sag v. 下垂,弯曲	03
polystyrene n. 聚苯乙烯	13	sandwich n. 夹层	13
polythene n. 聚乙烯	13	sanitary a. 卫生的	08
popularity * n. 普及,流行	16	sawtooth n. 锯齿(形状)	13
porosity n. 孔隙度,多空性	10	scientifically ad. 科学地	15
porous * a. 多孔的,有气孔的,能		sectional * a. 部分的,截面的	01

词	词性	释义	课次
serviceability	n.	功能,耐用性	06
settlement	n.	沉降,沉积	04
sewage	n.	污水	08
shaft *	n.	轴,杆状物	01
shipment	n.	装运,装载	09
shoddiest	a.	质量差的	08
simulate *	v.	假装,模拟	06
slab *	n.	平板,厚板	06
slake	vt.	(使石灰)熟化	09
slipshod	a.	马虎的,潦草的	08
sloppy	a.	湿透的,水多的,滑稀的	10
software *	n.	软件	06
solidly	ad.	紧密地,坚固地	11
spatially	ad.	空间地	05
specifically	ad.	特定地,具体地	01
speculative	a.	投机的	08
sprinkler	n.	洒,喷淋	08
standby	a.	备用的,辅助的	
statical	a.	静止的,固定的	04
statistically	ad.	统计(学)地	14
statute	n.	法规	08
stave	n.	桶板	08
strain	n.	应变,变形	14
strain harden		应变强化	02
structural	a.	结构的	01
stucco	n.	灰泥	11
subassembly	n.	组件,部件	06
submerged	a.	浸在水中的	01
subregion	n.	子结构,子域	16
substantially	ad.	大量的	11
substructure	n.	基础,下部结构	12
sufficiency	n.	足够的分量,充足	15
superpose	vt.	叠加	14
superposition *	n.	重合,叠加	04
superstructure	n.	上层建筑,上部结构	12
supervise	v.	监督,管理	13
supervision	n.	监督	07
susceptible *	a.	易受影响的	06
tarred felt		油毡	13
technological	a.	技术的,工艺的	12
temperate	a.	(气候等)温和的,适度的	13
tenement	n.	住屋,一套房间	08
tensile *	a.	拉力的,拉伸的	01
texture *	n.	纹理	07
theoretically	ad.	理论上地	15
thereafter *	ad.	由此	08
thermal *	a.	热的,热量的	13
thermodynamics *	n.	热力学	03
tile	n.	瓦片	11
tint	vt.	给…染色	13
torque *	n.	扭矩,转矩	03
torsion *	n.	扭转	15
transit-mixed *	a.	混合运输的	07
transition *	n.	转变,过渡	02
translucent	a.	半透明的	13
transverse *	a.	横向的,横断的	15
trivial *	a.	无足轻重的	16
troughed	a.	槽型的	13
trowel	n.	瓦刀	11
truss	n.	构架,桁架	15
tuff	n.	凝灰岩	09
ultimate	a.	极限的,最后的	02
ultimate	n.,a.	极限;极限的	06
unavoidable *	a.	不可避免的	13
undervalue	vt.	低估,轻视	15
uniform	a.	均匀的	01
unimpaired	a.	未受损伤的	11
unobstructed	a.	没有障碍的,没有阻挡的	05
unpleasantness	n.	不愉快	13
vapour barrier		隔汽层	13
ventilate *	v.	使通风,换气	12
ventilation	n.	通风	13
versed	a.	精通的	06
vicinity *	n.	地区,近处	09
visualize *	v.	(使)形象化	03

void *	n. 孔隙,空洞,空隙		10
volcanic	a. 火山的		09
whereas *	conj. 而,却,反之		02
workability	n. 和易性		11
workable *	a. 有和易性的,可操作的		10
workstation	n. 工作站		16
zigzag	a. 锯齿状的,之(Z)字形的		11

Appendix II Translation for Reference

第 1 单元

材料力学引言

材料力学是应用力学的一个分支,它讨论固体在承受各种荷载时的性能。它是以"材料强度"和"变形体力学"等不同的名称为人们所熟知的研究领域。本书所讨论的固体包括承受轴向荷载的杆、轴、梁和柱,以及由这些部件组合的结构物。通常,我们分析的目的是要确定由于荷载所产生的应力、应变和变形;如果对于破坏荷载前的各荷载值都能求得应力、应变和变形的大小,我们就能对物体的力学性能得到完整的概念。

理论分析和实验结果在材料力学研究中具有同等重要的地位。在很多情况下,我们采取逻辑推导得到预示力学性能的公式和方程。但是,必须承认,除非已经知道材料的某些性质,否则这些公式是不能实际应用的,而这些性质又只有在实验室做了相应的试验后,我们才会知道。同样,工程中的许多重要问题不能借助于理论手段去有效地处理,因而实验测定就成为实践的需要了。材料力学的历史发展是理论和实验两者最好的结合。在某些情况下,试验导致有益的成果,而在另一些情况下,理论又会做到这一点。著名的人物如达·芬奇(1452—1519)和伽利略(1564—1642)虽然没有按今天的标准提出充分的理论去解释他们的实验结果,但他们用实验确定了金属线、杆和梁的强度。相反,著名数学家欧拉(1707—1783)早在 1744 年就提出了柱的数学理论并计算了柱的临界荷载,但很长时间内一直没有实验证明他所得出的结果的重要意义。所以欧拉的理论成果多年来未曾得到应用,但是今天它已成为柱的理论基础。

随着对本课程的学习,理论推导与实验确定材料性质相结合的重要性将会越加明显。本文将先讨论某些基本概念,如应力和应变,然后将研究承受拉伸、压缩和剪切的简单结构构件的性能。

应力和应变的概念可借等直杆的拉伸(图 1-1a)进行初步阐述。等直杆是在整个长度上具有等截面,并具有直轴线的杆件。该图中,假设轴向力 P 作用于轴的两端,使杆产生均匀的伸长或拉伸。与杆轴线成正交作一人为的截面 mm,将杆件分离出一部分成为隔离体(图 1-1b)。其右端受拉力 P 的作用,而其另一端的力代表杆件移去部分对留下部分的作用力。这些力沿整个横截面连续分布,类似于浸没面上液体静压力的连续分布。该力的集度,亦即单位面积上的力,称为应力,通常用希腊字母 σ 来表示。假设应力在整个横截面上均匀分布,我们可以很容易地看出其合力等于集度 σ 乘以杆的横截面积 A。此外,根据图 1-1b 所示物体的平衡,我们还可以看出此合力必定与力 P 的大小相等而方向相反。因此可得等直杆中均匀应力的方程:

$$\sigma = \frac{P}{A} \tag{1-1}$$

该方程说明应力的单位为力除以面积的单位，例如磅/平方英寸或千磅/平方英寸。如图所示，当杆被力 P 拉伸时，所产生的应力为拉应力；如果力反转其方向，使杆压缩，所产生的应力则称为压应力。

方程（1-1）能够成立的必要条件是：应力 σ 在杆的整个横截面上必须是均匀的。如果轴向力 P 通过横截面的形心，那么，此条件即会存在，这点可借静力学来证明。当荷载 P 不作用于形心处时，杆将产生弯曲，就需要作较为复杂的分析。但本书通篇假设所有轴向力均作用于横截面的形心处，除非特殊说明相反情况。同样，除非另有说明，一般均假设物体本身重量忽略不计，在讨论图 1-1 中的杆件时，就是这样假定的。

承受轴向力的杆件，其总伸长量用希腊字母 δ 来表示（图 1-1a），单位长度的伸长量，或应变，用下列方程来确定：

$$\varepsilon = \frac{\delta}{L} \tag{1-2}$$

式中 L 为杆的总长度。注意，应变 ε 为一无量纲的量。只要应变沿整个杆长是均匀的，就可按方程（1-2）求得其精确值。如果杆件受拉，其应变为拉伸应变，它表示材料伸长或拉伸；如果杆件受压，其应变则为压缩应变，它表示杆件的相邻横截面彼此移近。

第 2 单元

拉 伸 试 验

特定材料的应力和应变关系是由拉伸试验来确定的。材料的试件通常做成圆杆并置于试验机上进行拉伸，随着荷载的增加测出作用在试件上的外力和试件的伸长。把作用在试件上的拉力除以杆的横截面面积可得应力；把试件的伸长除以沿伸长方向的长度可得应变。通过这种方式可以得到材料的完整应力-应变图。

结构钢的应力—应变图的典型曲线如图 2-1a 所示，其中横轴表示轴向应变，由曲线 $OABCDE$ 的纵坐标来给出所对应的应力。从 O 点到 A 点应力和应变成正比关系，曲线是直线。过 A 点之后，应力和应变的线性关系不再存在。所以，A 点的应力叫做比例极限。对于低碳（结构）钢来说，比例极限通常在 30,000 psi（磅/英寸^2）到 36,000（磅/英寸^2），但对高强度钢来讲，此值就高得多。随着荷载的增加，应变的增长比应力快得多，直到 B 点出现相当大的伸长，而拉力不再增加，这种现象称之为材料的屈服。在 B 点的应力叫做屈服点或屈服应力。在 BC 段，材料变成塑性的，并且，试件实际产生的塑性变形量是比例极限时变形量的 10 到 15 倍。在 C 点，材料开始产生应变强化，对荷载的增加呈现出附加抗力。这样随着试件的伸长应力继续增加，直到 D 点，达到最大值，或称极限应力，超出该点，继续拉伸试件将出现荷载的减少，直到图中的 E 点产生试件断裂。

随着试件的伸长，产生侧向收缩，从而造成了试件横截面积的减少，这种现象在 C 点以前对应力-应变图没有影响。然而，在 C 点以后，随着横截面积的进一步减少，会对应力值的计算产生显著的影响。这时发生了明显的颈缩现象（如图 2-2）。如果用颈缩处实际横截面积计算 σ，则会发现实际的应力-应变曲线将沿着虚线 CE'。但是相反，超过极限应力后（DE 线），试件承受的总荷载实际上则减少，这是由于横截面积的减少而不是材料本身的强度降低所造成的。实际上材料承受应力一直增加到断裂点为止。然而在许多应用场合，基于试件的初始横截面面积，一般的应力-应变曲线 $OABCDE$，可为设计提供满意的信息。

在图 2-1a 中，画出了钢的应力-应变曲线的基本特性，但是这比例并不是真实的。因为，正如前所述，从 B 点到 C 点所产生的应变比从 O 点到 A 点的应变大 15 倍，并且从 C 点到 E 点的应变也远远大于 B 点到 C 点的应变。用正确比例绘制的曲线如图 2-1b，从图中可以看出，从 O 点到 A 点的应变与 A 点到 E 点的应变相比，非常小，几乎看不到，图的直线部分表现为垂直线。

钢材是当今普遍使用的结构材料，似乎只有钢材在出现明显的屈服点之后才发生明显的塑性应变。铝合金从线性段过渡到非线性段更加缓慢，其应力-应变图如图 2-3 所示。不论是钢还是铝合金，在断裂前都要经历大的应变，所以把它们归类于延性材料。在另一方面，脆性材料在相对低的应变值下断裂（如图 2-4），例如陶瓷、铸铁、混凝土、某些金属合金及玻璃。

与这些拉伸曲线类似，还可以获得各种材料压缩时的应力-应变曲线。并且还可得到比例极限、屈服点和强度极限等特征应力。对于钢材，可以发现拉伸和压缩的比例极限和屈服应力几乎是一样的。当然，对许多脆性材料来讲，在压缩时的特征应力比拉伸时大得多。

第 3 单元

材料力学的应用和学习方法

在所有的工程建设中，对结构的构件必须确定出其明确的外形尺寸。而且尺寸必须合理以抵抗作用在它们上面的实际的或可能的外力。因此，压力容器的壁必须具有足够强度以承受内压力。楼房的楼板必须按预期目的建造得足够坚固；机器的轴必须具有一定的尺寸以承受所需的扭矩；机翼必须具有安全地承受飞机在飞行或降落时空气对它产生的空气动力荷载的能力。同样地，复合结构的每一部分都必须有足够的刚度，使它们在荷载作用下，使用中不致于产生过大的变位或挠度。楼房的楼盖可能具有足够的强度，但也许会产生过大的变位。在有些情况下会引起制造设备的错位，而在另一些场合会导致楼板下抹灰天棚的开裂。同样，一个构件也许太薄或太细长以致于在压力作用下会因屈曲而失稳。也就是构件的初始形状可能变得不稳定。确定细长柱在屈曲之前承受最大荷载的能力或确定容器保持真空的安全水平具有重要的实际意义。

在工程实践中，常会遇到对给定材料的最低消耗问题。有时在卫星设计中，除了成本外，整个设计的可行性和成功与否取决于机体的重量。材料力学在过去，人们传统上把它叫做材料强度，其主要内容是研究构件在各种荷载作用下强度、刚度（变形特征）和稳定性的分析方法。换言之，这门课程可以称为可变形固体力学。

材料力学是一门相当古老的学科，通常认为起源于十七世纪初伽利略的著作中。在伽利略对荷载作用下固体特性的研究之前，建设者们遵循的是先例和经验的准则。伽利略是第一位试图在合理的基础上解释在荷载作用下一些构件性能的人。他研究了受拉和受压杆件，并且特别研究了在意大利海军军舰外壳中使用的梁。当然，从那以后在这方面已经取得了很大进展。必须注意，这一学科的发展很多都应归功于法国的研究者们，他们当中有一些杰出人物，象十九世纪初进行这项研究的库仑、泊松、纳维尔、圣维南还有柯西，他们在这一学科里做出了不可磨灭的贡献。

材料力学这门学科在工程领域所有分支都有许多重要应用。海洋结构设计者们需要它的方法；从事桥梁和建筑设计的土木工程师需要它的方法；采矿工程师和建筑工程师也是一样，他们都对结构感兴趣，原子能工程师在反应堆部件设计中也需要它的方法；机械工程师和化学工程师依赖这一学科的方法设计机器和压力容器；冶金学家们需要这一学科的基本概念来弄清楚怎样进一步改进现有材料；最后，电气工程师也需要它的方法。这是因为在电器设备很多部件的机械工程方面材料力学的方法是很重要的。材料力学中的方法都具有它本身的特性，它是一门特定的学科，也是工程学全部课程中最基础的课程之一。和它齐名的还有其他的基础学科，象流体力学、热力学和基础电学。

受到外力作用杆件的性能不仅依赖于控制力平衡的牛顿力学基本定律，而且还依赖于制造杆件材料的物理性质。与后者有关的必要信息来自实验室，在实验室里材料受到精确的已知外力作用，并且特别仔细地观察试件产生的断裂、变形等现象。这种现象的研究是这门课程的主要部分之一，但材料力学中的这一领域留给其他书籍讨论。在此我们感兴趣的是研究结果，并且本门课程与实验不同，是讨论理论分析或数学方法部分。根据以上理由，可见材料力学是一门实验与分析力学中牛顿定律相结合的科学。而来自后者的科学分支——静力学是本书读者熟悉的题目，也是本书的基础。

本教材仅限于材料力学中的简单问题。尽管我们所采用的方法比较简单，但由此得到的技术对于很多重要技术问题都是极为有用的。

通过求解大量习题可以很好地掌握本课程的主要内容。用材料力学方法分析和设计结构及机械构件所需要的公式不多，但学生通过本门课程的学习，一定会培养观察问题的能力和对计算数值本质的认识能力。对所求解的问题仔细完整地画出示意图对较快较完整地掌握本门课程是大有好处的。

第 4 单元

力法和位移法的描述

力法

1. 首先，需要确定超静定次数。放松次数应与超静定次数相同，每个放松都由解除一个外力或内力产生。放松时应使剩余结构是稳定的和静定的。然而在某些情况下，放松的数目可以小于超静定次数，只要剩余的超静定结构容易分析即可。在所有情况下，对这种也称为赘余力的放松力应仔细选择，以便放松后的结构易于分析。

2. 放松导致位移的不协调，第二步应确定放松结构中的这些不协调量或"误差"。换言之，计算对应于赘余力方向的位移"误差"的大小。这些位移可能是由于外加荷载、支座沉降或温度改变而造成的。

3. 第三步确定由于单位赘余力值而引起的在放松结构中的位移。这些位移要求与在第二步中算出的位移误差位置相同和方向相同。

4. 现在确定消除位移误差所必需的赘余力的值。这需要写出叠加方程，其中每个赘余力的影响都累加到放松结构的位移中。

5. 由此，我们得到作用在原始超静定结构上的力：它们是校正力（赘余力）和作用在放松结构上的力的总和。

位移法

位移法和力法的数学表达式类似。但是从计算工作量来看，其中一种或另一种方法可能更可取。

位移法可用于静定或超静定结构，但是它对于后者更有用，特别是当超静定次数很高时。

1. 首先，必须求出独立位移的数目。然后建立一个坐标系，确定结点位移的位置和方向。在坐标系中引入数目等于独立位移数的约束以防止结点位移的发生。有时，引入的约束数可能小于独立位移数，只要对所生成结构的分析是标准的并为大家所了解即可。

我们应注意，与力法不同，上述过程不需要对约束力进行选择。这个事实有助于位移法在通用计算机结构分析程序中的应用。

2. 现在，用汇交于一点的各杆件固端力的和来确定约束力。在大多数实际分析中，固端力可借助标准表格计算。

我们应记住约束力是用来防止在各种因素作用下在坐标处发生位移的，这些因素有外荷载、温度变化、或预应变，而这些因素可分别考虑或一起考虑。

如果分析是针对结构中一个结点位移的影响，例如一个支座的沉降，那么保持该结点位移所需的坐标处的力应包含在约束力中。

也应在需要的地方确定带有约束位置的节点的各构件内力。

3. 现在，假定结构中的一个坐标处的位移等于1，而所有其他坐标处的位移为零，确定结构保持这一状态所受的力。这些力作用在代表自由度的坐标处。确定这种变形状态下所要求位置的内力。对应每个坐标处的单位位移，重复进行这个过程。

4. 确定消除（2）中引入的约束力所必需的位移值。这需要叠加方程，在方程中把每个位移对约束力的效应进行叠加。

5. 最后，通过将作用于被约束结构上的力和第四步由于结点位移产生的力相加便得出作用在原结构上的力。

第 5 单元

建 筑 结 构

就工程的实质而言，建筑结构可定义为：以保持形状和稳定为目的的各个基本构件的组合体。其基本目的是抵抗作用在建筑物上的各种荷载并把它传到地基上。

从建筑学的角度来讲，建筑结构并非仅仅如此。它与建筑风格是不可分割的，在不同程度上是一种建筑风格的体现。如能巧妙地设计建筑结构，则可建立或加强建筑空间与建筑平面之间的格调与节奏。它在直观上可以是显性的或隐性的。它能产生和谐体或对照体。它可能既局限又开放。不幸的是在一些情况下，它不能被忽视。它是实际存在的。

结构设计还必须与建筑风格相吻合。物理学和数学的原理及工具为区分在结构上的合理和不合理的形式提供了依据。艺术家有时可以不必考虑科学就能画出图形，但建筑师却不行。

在建筑结构中至少应包括三项内容：

稳定性

强度和刚度

经济性

在上述三项要求中，首先是稳定性。它在保持建筑物形状上是必不可少的。一座不稳定的建筑结构意味着有不平衡的力或失去平衡状态，并且由此导致建筑结构整体或构件产生加速度。

强度的要求意味着所选择的用以承受由荷载产生的应力的结构材料和结构形状都必须适当。实际上，通常都提供一个安全系数以便在预计的荷载作用下，所使用材料的应力不会接近破坏应力。被称为刚度的材料的特性，需与强度要求一起考虑。刚度不同于强度，因为它涉及荷载作用下结构应变的大小和变形的程度。具有很高强度。但刚度较低的材料，在外力作用下会因变形过大而失去其使用价值。

建筑结构的经济性指的不仅仅是所用材料的费用。建筑经济是一个复杂的问题，其中包括原材料、制作、安装和维修。必须考虑设计和施工中人工费及能源消耗的费用。施工的速度和工程成本（利息）也是需要考虑的因素。对大多数设计情况，不能仅仅考虑一种建筑材料，经常存在一些有竞争性的选择，而具体应选择那种并不明显。

除了这三种最基本要求之外，其他几种因素也值得重视。首先，结构或结构体系必须和建筑物的功能相吻合而不应该与建筑风格相矛盾。例如，线性功能要求线性结构，所以把保龄球场的顶部盖成圆形是不合适的。剧院必须是较大跨度、中间没有障碍的结构，而高档饭店却不是这样。简而言之，结构必须具备合适的维护空间的功能。

第二，结构必须防火，很显然，至少一直到内部人员安全撤离为止，结构体系必须能保持完整。建筑规范详细规定了建筑物的某些构件抵抗热量而不倒坍的时间。用于那些构件的结构材料必须自身具有防火性或者用耐火材料加以适当保护。所规定的防火等级将取决于一系列因素，它包括建筑空间的占有和使用；建筑物的尺寸及建筑物的位置。

第三，结构应与建筑物的循环系统很好地结合。它不应与给排水管道，通风系统或人的活动空间相矛盾（这是最重要的）。很显然，各种建筑系统在设计时必须相互协调。对任何一个系统的设计，可以有顺序地一步一步地进行，而对所有系统的设计则采用并行方式来完成。从空间上来讲，在一座建筑物中所有的构件之间都是相互依存的。

第四，结构在心理上及外观上必须给人一种安全感。在风载作用下晃动得很厉害的高层框架虽然没有危害，但仍然不适宜居住。弹性太大的轻质楼盖系统可能给居住者很不舒适的感觉。没有窗棂的巨大玻璃窗户尽管是相当安全的，但对居住在楼房里的人来说，特别是当他站在临街40层高楼的大玻璃窗前时，总会感到极不安全。

有时建筑师必须有意采取积极措施来增加建筑结构外表的强度和坚固性。外观的安全性也许比真实表达建筑结构更重要，因为没有受过训练的人是不能分清真实的和感觉中的安全性的。

第6单元

结构分析的目的、结构模型以及分析与结构设计的关系

结构分析是确定在给定荷载下结构中产生的力和变形以便使结构设计得合理并能检查现有结构的安全状况。

在结构设计中，必须先从结构的概念开始拟定一种结构形式，然后再进行分析。这样做 能确定构件的尺寸以及所需要的钢筋，以便 a) 承受设计荷载而不出现损坏或过大变形，（在正常使用或工作状态）；b) 防止在规定的超载施加到结构上以前倒塌（安全性或极限状况）。

由于通常在工作荷载作用下，结构处于弹性状态，因此以弹性状态假设为基础的结构理论就适用于正常状态。结构的倒塌通常在远远超出材料弹性范围，超出临界点后才会发生，因而建立在材料非弹性状态基础上的极限强度理论是合理确定结构安全性，防止倒塌所必需的。不过弹性理论可用来确定延性结构强度的安全近似值（塑性下限逼近法），在钢筋混凝土设计中通常采用这种方法。基于这种原因，在本章中仅仅采用结构的弹性理论。

结构模型

仔细地观察所有结构都是三维构件的组合体，对其进行精确的分析，甚至在理想状态下，也是一个棘手的工作，即使专业人员也无从考虑。由于这种原因，分析人员工作的一个重要部分是将实际结构和荷载状态简化成一个易于合理分析的模型。

这样，结构框架系统可分解成板和楼盖梁，楼盖梁是由立柱支撑的交叉梁系，立柱将荷载传递到基础上。因为传统的结构分析不能分析板的作用，所以经常理想化成类似于梁的条形系统。同样，普通的方法不能处理三维框架系统，因此利用平面结构组合系统建立整个结构的模型，分别加以分析。现代的矩阵——计算机法可以分析整个系统从而革新了结构分析，这样可对荷载作用下结构的性能作出更可靠的预测。

实际荷载状态也是很难确定和很难客观表达的，为了进行分析，必须进行简化。例如，桥梁结构上的交通荷载主要是动力的和随机性的，通常理想化成静态行驶的标准卡车或分布荷载，以用来模拟实际产生的最危险的荷载状态。

同样，连续梁有时简化为简支梁，刚性结点简化为铰接点，忽略填充墙，把剪力墙当成梁；在决定如何建立一个结构模型使之比较客观，但又比较简单时，分析人员必须记住每个这样的理想化都将使所求的解更加可疑。分析得越客观，产生的信心越大，所取的安全系数（或忽略的因素）可以越小。这样，除非规范条款控制，工程师必须估算出结构精确分析比所需追加的费用与结构中可能节省的费用相比，是否合算。

结构分析的最重要的用处是在结构设计中作为一种工具。它通常是反复试算过程中的一个环节，在这种方法中，首先，在假定的恒载下对假定的结构体系进行分析，然后根据分析结果设计各构件。这个阶段称为初步设计，由于这种设计常常在变化，通常采用粗略的快速分析方法就足够了。在此阶段，估计结构的成本，修正荷载及构件特性，并对设计进行检查以便改进。至此，所作的更改已纳入到结构中，需进行更精细的分析，并修改构件设计。这种设计过程会收敛，收敛的速度取决于设计者的能力。很清楚，为了设计需要从"迅速而粗略"到"精确"的各种分析方法。

因而，有能力的分析人员必须掌握严密的分析方法，必须能够通过适当的假设条件进行简化分析，必须了解可利用的标准设计和分析手段以及建筑规范中允许的简化方法。同时，现代的分析人员必须精通结构矩阵分析的基本原理及其在数字计算机中的应用以及会应用现有的分析程序及有关软件。

第 7 单元

混凝土和钢筋混凝土的特性

混凝土是一种人造组合石材，主要由四种成分组成：波特兰水泥，水，砂子和粗骨料。水泥和水混合成水泥浆，将砂子和石子粘合在一起。理想的骨料级配应使泥浆的体积最小，仅将每块骨料包上薄薄的一层即可。大多数结构混凝土是碎石混凝土，但是轻质结构混凝土（大约是碎石混凝土密度的 2/3）正日益得到普及。

混凝土基本上是一种几乎没有抗拉强度的抗压缩材料。所以，混凝土抗拉强度低也导致混凝土抗剪强度低。在产生拉伸应力和剪应力的部位加入钢筋克服了这些缺陷。在荷载作用下，钢筋混凝土梁实际上会有许多沿垂直于主拉应力方向的微裂缝。这些部位的拉力完全被钢筋所承担。

给定混凝土的抗压强度是其组成成分的质量和比例以及新浇混凝土的养护方法的函数。（养护是硬化过程，在此其间，必须防止混凝土过干，因为水分的存在是进行化学反应所必须的。）坚硬并具有良好级配的粗骨料对于优质混凝土是至关重要的。然而，决定其强度的最重要因素是其配料中的含水率。水泥适当水化需要最小量的水分。为了操作和浇筑混凝土需要多加一些水，但是过量的水分会导致强度明显降低。

由波特兰水泥协会出版的"混凝土混合物的设计与控制"一书中全部包含了这类以及其他一些论题。这是一本优秀的参考书，它涉及混凝土配料设计及适合的施工实践。美国混凝土学会出版了广泛采用的专用于钢筋混凝土结构要求的规范。

混凝土被认为是作"可成型的"或"可模性的"结构材料。与其他材料相比，混凝土易制成曲线型构件和各种曲面。混凝土没有固有的纹理，但它呈现其成模材料的纹理，因此混凝土可呈现各种各样的外观。制造混凝土无论原材料还是人工费都相当便宜，普通水泥的基本材料在世界各地都可得到。（然而，应注意的是混凝土所必需的钢筋在不发达国家可能不易得到。）

就这种材料的特性而言，钢筋混凝土最佳的结构用途是在那些要求连续性和刚性的建筑结构中。钢筋混凝土具有整体性，可自动实现固定连接或连续连接。这些抗弯结点使得许多低层混凝土建筑物在横向荷载作用下不需要辅助斜支撑系统。实质上混凝土梁与混凝土柱的连接与钢和木构件的连接大不一样，聪明的设计人员是不会忽视这种差异的。（这些要点不适合于预制结构件，这些预制结构件通常不以连续方式连接。）

混凝土本身是耐火的，不需要单独的保护系统。由于它的质量，混凝土也可用作为有效的隔声材料。

从缺点方面考虑，遗憾的是混凝土相当重，经常可见有混凝土结构仅支撑它本身重量就要消耗了它大部分的承载能力。制造低密度而保持其高性能水准的混凝土通常会导致成本提高。不过，使用轻质混凝土有时能产生综合经济效益。

混凝土比大多数其他建筑材料需要更多的质量监督。现代化的输送搅拌混凝土的供应厂商遍布美国各城市，其混合物通常具有均匀的高质量。然而，现场或临时搅拌的混凝土需要技术性的监督。无论在何种混凝土的施工中漏加钢筋或放错钢筋位置都会导致构件承载能力降低。无论是操作或养护条件不好或二者兼而有之都能严重削弱混凝土的强度。由于种种原因，大多数建筑规范都要求在施工的各个阶段进行独立的现场检查。

适当的混凝土浇筑也多少取决于周围气候条件。更重要的是，过高的温度以及低于（或接近于）冰点的温度都能使混凝土施工非常困难。

第 8 单元

建 筑 规 范

建筑规范是用详细的条例形式制定的法规。这个法规是由一个市政当局或其他政府机构制定的。其目的是为了确保在所管辖范围之内的所有建筑物符合一定的卫生或安全的最起码的标准。在政府的固有权力当中，建筑规范具有法定权力，这种权力是为了保护其公民免受不卫生或不安全的环境而给他们带来可能出现的危害。

因此，建筑规范涉及下列内容：建筑结构的合理性；所用材料的质量和强度；良好的工艺；正确地安装合格的电线及设备；正确地安装合格的燃气、煤和燃油的供暖设备及它们所使用的管道，正确地铺设合格的卫生设施及管道；合理使用耐火材料及正确设置防火安全门。

在大部分市政管理中，所有新的建设计划在施工开始之前必须由有关建筑部门的官员审核批准。同时，这些审核官员有权随时到拟建的地段检查。在建筑场地批准使用之前，他们有权检查全部设备、材料及工艺。如果设备、工艺或材料不符合建筑规范的标准，他们颁布施工许可之前，有权命令进行必要的改动。

一旦一个建筑项目获得批准并开工，假如建筑商在开工之后，可能想要在电力、供热或管道系统进行根本性的变更，或在结构上进行根本性改动，建筑部门必须预先审核批准这些变动，并且检查工艺和材料是否也作相应的改动。如果一项工程是由合格的电工或管道工完成，可以认为所采用的施工工艺和材料都是适当的，尽管建筑部门总是保留随后检查及下达认为必要修改的命令的权利。

促进建筑规范发展的动力是基于人道主义角度来考虑的。如果没有规范强加的法律限制，就不能防止建筑商建成最廉价的、质量最差的、十分拥挤的住宅群之后逃脱惩罚。也许在美国众所周知的偷工减料的建筑施工例子就是"冷水公寓"——旧法律公寓，这类公寓一度曾经布满整个曼哈顿较低的东部地区和纽约市的许多其他地区。在这些公寓当中存在着拥挤和不卫生情况。由于上述这些原因，造成了大量的火灾。由此导致了建筑规范的采用和发展。

被美国许多大中城市所采用的建筑规范是集工程知识、当地的建筑习俗及与当地政治现实相适应的产物。起初，建筑规范是规定型的，它要求所有的建筑物都使用规定的材料，按规定的方法来施工。建筑商在材料和采用的施工方法上几乎没有选择的余地。这种规定型的建筑规范如何影响了纽约市的建筑风格，这里有一个出奇的例子。纽约市中所有的建筑物都要求用木制的屋顶水箱，并使其与洒水灭火设备相连。结果，任何一个从曼哈顿区中部的摩天大楼上往下观看的人都会为所看到的景象大吃一惊。在那全是钢筋和混凝土的顶部，极不协调地耸立着无数圆锥形屋顶的木制水箱。

当建筑商试图用他们能买到的最便宜的建筑材料，用最差的施工方式建造房屋时，规定型建筑规范是必不可少的。但是，现在时代不同了，新的材料层出不穷。自从第二次世界大战以来，性能型的建筑规范已是大势所趋。这种规范提出材料或结构的性能标准。建筑商都可以自由选择能满足这些标准的材料或建筑技术。

例如，规定型的规范会简单地规定房屋的下水道要用一定质量、一定尺寸的铸铁管，它还规定管子应该以规定的方式安装。管道工程的承包人在这个问题上既无选择余地，也无发言权。但是性能型的建筑规范则规定，管道应该不受污水或埋设管道土壤中的任何腐蚀物或有害物的损害，还规定管道应该符合某种最低强度的要求。此外，管道不应该受规定范围内温度变化的影响。管道工程承包人可以自由选用塑料管、铸铁管，或者如果他愿意的话还可以用黄金管，只要他能表明，管子的确符合当地规定标准即可。

第9单元

水泥与混凝土的早期历史

自从人类开始存在时起，人的住处一直要求应用每个时代所能提供的最好的技术。在最初时期，建筑物是由土夯实而成，或者在没有任何连接或粘接物的情况下，用石头一块一块地垒砌而成。石材建筑的稳定性依赖于重石块有规则的排放。最早的砖石建筑可能是由阳光晒干后的土砖，有规则地一层一层砌在薄泥浆上而构成。泥浆变干后，就成为坚实的土墙。这种建筑结构在世界上一些干燥的沙漠地区曾经很常见。

烧制过的石膏作为一种胶凝材料，最早产生于古埃及时期，并显然曾用于建造金字塔。后来，希腊人和罗马人发现了用石灰石来烧制生石灰，然后把它熟化制作灰泥的方法。希腊人和罗马人都懂得，用某种细土与石灰和砂子混合即可生产优质的胶凝材料。希腊人用的材料是一种取自圣多林岛的火山灰，至今仍在世界的那个地区使用。罗马人使用的胶凝材料中，最好的那种是取自维苏威山附近波佐利地区的一种火山灰。因此，直到现在，用于混凝土中的某种矿物掺合剂仍然称为火山灰。

罗马人生产的水泥是一种水硬水泥，就是说这种水泥在水的作用下会变硬。很多古罗马建筑都是用某种混凝土建造的，使用的就是这些材料，石材建筑物也是用含有类似成分的砂浆粘合的。

中世纪期间，调制优质砂浆的技术几乎失传，大约十一世纪达到最低点，那时使用的材料质量很差。后来石灰的质量开始改进，十四世纪或稍后，又开始使用火山灰水泥。

比较近期，最著名的工程项目之一是在1757～1759年间在英格兰海岸外面建造的新的涡石灯塔。该工程的设计师及工程师约翰·斯米顿为该建筑研究过多材料和多种粘结石块的方法。

那时工程学和科学研究开始迅猛发展。一些国家的研究人员当时都在研究用石膏、石灰石和其他天然材料制成的胶凝剂。通过烧制石灰与粘土的天然混合物来制造水泥的方法便是其中的一项发现。尽管这种天然水泥的使用继续了好多年，但由于天然材料的配比变化不定，使这种天然水泥的性能非常不稳定。

1824年，一位英国里兹的瓦匠约瑟夫·艾斯波丁取得了他称之为波特兰水泥的一种材料的专利权。之所以如此命名是因为用这种水泥制成的混凝土被认为很象是从英国波特兰附近采集来的石灰石。艾斯波丁被公认为发明了一种制造水泥的方法，先把石灰石与粘土按比例掺合在一起，放在高温中焙烧成熟料，再将熟料磨细即成为水硬水泥。他的小水泥窑每窑要烧几天时间，一次可生产大约16t熟料。水泥制造业的扩大与发展在其后的若干年相当缓慢。然而，大约在1850年，这门工业不仅在英国，而且在德国和比利时都已牢固确定。

水泥运销美国开始于1868年，大约在1895年达到高峰。此时美国的水泥生产也已初具规模。

在进口水泥的同时，由于修建伊利运河及其配套工程对水泥的需求，美国生产天然水泥在十九世纪初就已开始。其后，水泥回转窑的开发致使大规模的水泥生产遍及全世界。

铁路、桥梁、楼房的建设以及城市街道路面的铺设，使得混凝土的应用得以推广。用钢筋来增强混凝土的研究工作始于法国。1875年美国首次应用钢筋混凝土。这个时期大多数混凝土含水量很低，要用大量手工作业才能使之夯实就位。接着有一段时间使用湿混凝土，这种湿混凝土可以流淌就位。然而，许多混凝土的使用者认识到，使用湿混凝土是件蠢事。大约1920年，达夫·亚布拉姆斯公布了他的研究及观测结果。他说明：混凝土的质量直接受到用水量与水泥量之比的影响。在一定范围内，混凝土的质量随其水灰比的升高而降低。这已成为混凝土工艺的基本法则之一。

第10单元

混凝土的优缺点及其水灰比

混凝土是波特兰水泥、水、砂子与卵石或碎石的拌合物。水与水泥调制成水泥浆，在水泥浆中把砂子和碎石或卵石混合在一起。砂子和碎石或卵石共同构成混凝土拌合物的骨料。骨料不起结构作用，它仅仅是加入到水泥浆中来降低成本的一种填充物。骨料通常占一块特定混凝土体积的百分之七十五。劣质骨料可以极大地降低混凝土的强度，可是优质骨料对于增加水泥的强度却没有多大影响。

作为建筑材料，混凝土有两大主要优点，一是比较便宜，二是当它处于塑性状态时容易操作和浇注。混凝土的主要结构优点是它抗压强度高、耐久性能好。它能承受很高的压力荷载。这使它非常适用于建造基础、墙壁、楼房的支柱，也适用于修筑公路及街道。

混凝土的主要结构缺点是它抗拉强度低。就是说，它承受拉伸或弯曲荷载时容易断裂。因此，常常将钢筋埋入混凝土中。加固钢筋给混凝土提供了它所缺乏的抗拉强度。置入钢筋的混凝土叫做钢筋混凝土。

除了抗拉强度差之外，像大多数建筑材料一样，混凝土还会热胀冷缩，湿胀干缩。在施工中，如果这些胀缩运动超出允许限度，混凝土就会开裂。

与常识相反，硬化后的混凝土并不是不透水的。一些湿气会迁移到加工最好的混凝土中。在拌合中加入了太多的水会使混凝土内出现过多的气孔。万一这种现象出现，混凝土养护完后，湿气会很容易地进入其内。当冷天到来时，万一水分还存在于混凝土内，便会冻结，这会给建筑物带来严重的结冻损伤。

尽管混凝土有这些缺点，它仍不失为一种天生具有坚固与耐久性的建筑材料。如果水、水泥和骨料的比例经过认真计算，如果混凝土的浇注与养护按照简明的规章来进行，完全可能获得它固有的全部强度与耐久性。

混凝土的水灰比是它最终强度的决定因素。曾经有一段时间，混凝土的配料比例规定为1∶2∶4。它表示从体积上一份波特兰水泥、二份砂子和四份卵石拌合在一起，之后加入足够的水来获得和易性良好的拌合物。这种作业过程完全忽视了水灰比的重要性。其结果是经常调配出强度非常低的混凝土。因为就工人而言，自然倾向于多加水，足以使混凝土的浇注尽可能容易,越稀滑越好。这种规定混凝土成分比例的做法现已淘汰,不应该再遵循。

从理论上讲,仅有3加仑水便可完全水化1立方英尺水泥(1袋水泥正好1立方英尺,重94磅)。可是按照这种水灰比加工出来的拌合物太干不能操作。因此,在实践中需要再多加些水来获得和易性良好的拌合料,每袋水泥加水在4~8加仑之间为宜。

但是在水灰比中,水的比例越大,最终制成的混凝土的强度越低。为了得到和易性好的混凝土而需要多加入的水将随着混凝土的硬化从混凝土中蒸发掉,这将在混凝土内留下无数的气孔。这便是为什么在混凝土内总存在一些孔隙的原因。当超量的水使用后,就会产生超量的孔隙,这会使混凝土严重渗漏。万一当冷天到来,这些孔隙充满了水分,它们会引起上述的结冻损伤。

因此,作为一般规定,每袋水泥加入6加仑水应该被视为配制混凝土的最大加水量,并且所用的水量越少,混凝土强度越高。作为骨料组成部分的砂子所含表面水分也应包括在6加仑加水量之内。

第 11 单元

砂 浆

砂浆是一种胶凝材料(可能是硅酸盐水泥或石灰或是二者兼有)和砂子的混合物。当把水加入到这些成分中时,就形成了一种可塑性物质,这种物质可用来粘结砖、瓦、混凝土砌块和其他种类的砌块。砂浆硬化后,砌块就被砂浆牢牢地粘结起来,形成了一个结构单元。

砂浆与其他胶凝材料,如混凝土、熟石膏和灰泥有着密切的关系,但是若把砂浆和这些材料混同起来,或是想用这些材料来替代砂浆是错误的,因为每一种材料均具有各自的特点,互不相同。

由于"一环薄弱,全局必垮"的错误推论,人们普遍认为,要想使砌体结构坚固,砂浆也必须是坚固的。例如:熟悉混凝土的人常会推断,作为一种类似混凝土的胶凝材料,砂浆应具有与混凝土类似的特性,并应按照同样的方式进行调制和使用;又比如:既然混凝土有或是应该有很高的抗压强度,那么,砂浆也应该有很高的抗压强度。但是砂浆的主要作用是粘结砌块,而不是抵抗压力,也不是增加砌块的强度。

对由各种不同强度的砂浆建成的砖墙已经做了大量的实验。这些实验一致表明,当用来粘结砖块的砂浆比砖块的强度低时,砖墙的强度最高。实际上,在不影响结构整体强度的情况下,砂浆实质上可以比砖的强度低很多。只要砂浆强度能够抵抗天气和冻结水的侵蚀作用,它就坚固得足以用于一般外墙。

但为了论证,假定一面砖墙是用比砖的抗压强度还高的砂浆砌成的,这面墙所承受的任何应力——比如说由墙下土的沉陷而导致的应力,将导致砖块沿最大应力方向断裂,这种断裂将形成一条从墙顶到墙脚，贯穿墙体的锯齿状裂缝。

但是，当砂浆像应该的那样比砖的强度低时，结构中的任何应力将全部被砂浆所吸收，砂浆吸收这些应力后将形成许多肉眼看不见的微小裂缝，这样，结构的基本强度没有受到损坏，墙的整体外观及其结构的完整性不变。

然而，砌体结构还可能出现另一种断裂现象。有时应力是通过砂浆与砖的分离得以释放的，结果，沿着砖的砌筑模式穿过砂浆出现了锯齿形裂缝。由于在砌筑完好的砖墙中最不应出现的就是砌块与砂浆粘结薄弱，而导致砌块和砂浆粘结薄弱的是由于疏忽或是工艺较差，也可能是二者兼而有之，或是由于砂浆配合的比例和调制方法有误，或是由于向砖上抹砂浆方式不当，也可能是二者共同导致的结果。

以适当比例的水泥、石灰和砂子加入适量的水刚调制成的砂浆具有一种特性叫和易性，有时也称为可塑性。就像很难说明煎薄饼用的面糊或者软化了的奶油的稠度一样，砂浆的和易性很难用语言来描述，但不具备这一特点的新砂浆是不能将砌块紧紧地粘结在一起的。和易性好的砂浆，可用一把瓦刀毫不费力，光滑而均匀地涂抹在砌块表面上。砂浆具有粘性，当把砂浆涂抹在砖的侧面时，这一特性使砂浆能保持自身的形状，并防止由于自身的重量而坍落。和易性好的砂浆具有弹性，这就使泥瓦工能将砌块紧密地安装就位。从微观来看，可以说和易性好的砂浆和砌块表面接触极为紧密，因而使砂浆和砌块之间的粘结极为牢固。

第 12 单元

设计的一般依据

高层建筑结构的选择不仅仅依据对结构本身具体情况的了解，而且可能更多地取决于与文化、社会、经济及技术的要求有关的许多因素。必须记住，结构只是许多要考虑的问题中的一个。本文将讨论一些主要和高层建筑的技术设计有关的问题。

建筑师通常不得不迁就许多类型建筑物的目的——盈利。当他对设计过程的经济情况有更深的了解时，他就有可能增加创造更佳建筑风格的机会。

应该认识到的重要一点是：选择一种建筑体系不应当仅仅靠先入为主的偏爱；相反，还应该包括对经济因素的周密考虑。因此，对某一特定的建筑物可能提出两种或两种以上的建造方法，这些方法看起来甚至很相似，但通常总有一种体系建造起来更经济。

一个设计人员必须考虑的，不仅仅是建造这项工程需要多少投资，还要考虑建成项目的经营管理所需费用多少；他势必要涉及建筑经济。随着建筑物高度的增加，结构、机械系统及电梯需要越来越多的空间。这样，所剩余的出租空间就更少了。不仅如此，随着高度的增加，电梯和机械系统的造价也在增加。同样的道理也适用于承包商的费用。因为建筑物增高了，需要更加高级的施工设备。但是所有这些增加的费用可以靠高的地价和在特定位置上对建筑物的需求来弥补。随着建筑物高度的增加，每平方英尺楼面面积的地价显著降低。同样，管理费用减少了。因为管理一幢大建筑物和管理若干小型结构相比，每平方英尺的费用较少。

现在已经开始依靠计算机来准确估算高层建筑的这些复杂的经济问题，因为要弄清现代摩天大楼所牵涉到的一切因素以及每个因素的全部细节已经超出人的计算能力了。

在一个项目的设计和制图阶段，建筑师、工程师和承包人的配合协作将增大求得经济解决办法的可能。这种集体的努力使得在最后图纸全部画完之前就有可能开始建筑施工。施工开始得越早，建筑物在施工费用上涨方面就节约了开支，而且获益也就越早。

建筑物的使用情况有赖于它基础下面土的强度。基础（或称下部结构）将上部结构与土联系起来。基础接受并分布荷载以便基土能承受这些荷载。建筑物型式的选择在很大程度上取决于现场的地质情况。在确定任何结构体系之前，必须对土的状况进行调查，以便预知结构的工作情况。举个例子，如果在一特定地点，土的承载能力很低，可能需要桩或沉箱以取得适当的地基支承。在这种情况下，混凝土这种重型材料的建筑物比轻的钢结构造价可能要高得多。总之，建筑结构的三个参数——上部结构、下部结构和土——在选择结构体系方面尚留有若干余地可供组合搭配。

制作与建造程序的规划可以表明与选择建筑体系有关的一些重要因素。在选择预制装配施工方法时，这些因素确实可作为主要依据。采用这些建筑体系可以减少劳动力费用和建造时间。在设计时应考虑尽量减少结构部件数目以缩短施工时间；避免使用复杂的封闭式类型；并把工地焊接限制在最小范围内。而且，在选择施工方法之前，必须了解制作与建造程序。

机械系统包括供热、通风、空调、电梯、电、管道和废物处理等装置，其平均造价占高层建筑物总造价的三分之一以上。这一重要的经济因素清楚地说明了对建筑体系的选择必须考虑到建筑物的设施造价。供能系统可集中设置在与建筑物总核心区结合在一起的机械核心区中。有时个别管道空间也可布置在外立面。对于某些大型供能要求的建筑物，有时可以采用带机械层的空间体系。所有这些方法对于建筑物的整体外观和结构体系经济效益的选择均有重要作用。

第 13 单元

厂 房 设 计

厂房设计因其包含许多重要设施的设计而使绝大多数土木工程师感兴趣。在厂房设计中，工程师是主要的设计者，不象在多层建筑的设计中他只是个助手。他必须设计道路、排水，或许还要设计供水、供暖或空调，设置电力和电话电缆及煤气管道。如果可能，他起码会争取在主要施工开始之前把主要道路和排水管道铺设好。这使得在工地上通行要容易得多。而保持工地干燥一些，多半能减少车辆的损坏。

如果是单层厂房，除热带地区外，通常可以从屋顶得到充分光照，但是如果厂房不止一层，任何大跨度建筑物内底层的天然采光就很困难，或者完全不可能。由于这个缘故，美国的一些厂房设计人员建造了没有窗户的厂房，全部采用空调。而且随着跨数增大，中部的房间无窗户而全靠空调的现象将是无法避免的。事实上，现在把卫生间设在房子中部的做法已经很普遍。这样，便不会浪费装设窗户的可贵位置，而窗户对起居室用处会更大。温带地区的空调设备应设计成夏天送冷气，而冬天送暖气。

屋顶采光可以在普通的薄板斜面屋顶上通过透明板，或通过锯齿形屋顶实施。锯齿形屋顶在北半球朝北，而在南半球朝南。采光屋顶使光线或垂直下射，或投射在屋顶斜坡上，并提供良好的通风条件。玻璃仍然是透光的常用材料，因为它最便宜。不过在热带国家它并不适用。在薄板屋顶上少量板材可用透明或半透明材料代替，或者用半透明的玻璃纤维，或者用透明的塑料（无色或染成红、黄等色）。所有这些大型薄板都可制成波纹状，使它们能跨越大约2米的距离。

厂房施工，常常为数百米长的大跨单层厂房的设计和施工是土木工程师的一项典型工作。虽然经常由建筑师来对这类工程进行监理，但通常是由建筑师和工程设计师共同了解委托人的需要，努力协作，才能使工程顺利进行。

对于无噪声的轻工业厂房，屋顶被覆通常采用工厂制造的板材，其种类现有几百种之多。它们可加工成波纹状或槽形，或平板，材料有钢板，胶合板，铝板，或者石棉水泥板。其外部防水层也可使用铜板，油毡或钢板。有些被覆造价很高，特别是那些夹层中含有高效隔热层的，如膨胀聚苯乙烯或玻璃纤维的。

隔热层必须完全防止冷绝缘材料的较热面外的空气中水分凝结。这样在天气热的情况下，冷凝水将出现在绝缘体的内层。而在寒冷的天气，冷凝水将出现在外层。隔热层必须严格防湿，否则潮气进入后，隔热效能将失去作用。随着隔热效果的丧失，冷凝作用将增加，并将进入更多的潮气，直至隔热效果完全丧失，更不用说阻挡墙上的令人讨厌的潮湿了。

为此不仅需要防湿，而且必须防止空气进入隔热层。这个任务可由聚乙烯、金属或其他材料制成的防水板，叫做隔汽层来完成。隔汽层接缝处必须密封好，以防止空气渗入而引起水凝结。土木工程师应先了解被覆层适用于炎热气候或寒冷气候，而制造商通常很乐于向可能的买主提供全部信息。

对于噪声大的厂房，如生产重型机械的厂房（汽车制造厂等），因为噪声可穿透，被覆板块就不适用。这时使用重墙就更理想，因为隔声效能和墙的重量有关。过去英国全部使用砖墙。而现代土木工程承包商使用4～5m长的水泥预制构件，通过大型吊车安装。如果工地设置安排合理，有合适的吊车可达到架起构件的高度，这种墙很快就可造好。如果构件太大，一部吊车不够，可用两部吊车同时工作。另外的办法就是降低墙板（构件）单元的高度，使其长度保持与柱距相符。这种结构简单，外型美观。如果吊车过小，构件只有15cm高，可以考虑在构件接缝处砌一薄层灰浆来挡风。如果构件大，接缝少，这种灰浆接缝就没有太大意义了。

第 14 单元

结构动力分析的主要目的

本书的主要目的是：介绍任何给定型式的结构在承受任意动荷载时所产生的应力和挠度的分析方法。从某种意义上讲，这个目的可以认为是，把通常只适用于静荷载的结构分析标准方法加以推广，使之也可以在动荷载的分析中加以应用。对此，静荷载可以被看作仅仅是动荷载的一种特殊形式。然而，在线性结构分析中，更为方便的是区分施加荷载中的静力和动力分量，然后分别计算对每种荷载的反应，最后将两个反应分量叠加得出总效应，当进行这样处理时，静力的和动力的分析方法在性质上是根本不同的。

为了上述目的，"动力的"或"动的"这个词可以简单地被定义为随时间而改变的，这样，动荷载就是大小、方向、作用点随时间而改变的任何荷载。同样，动荷载下的结构反应，即所产生的挠度及应力，也是随时间而改变的或"动的"。

计算动荷载下的结构反应有两种基本不同的方法：确定的和非确定的。在任何给定的情况下，究竟选取哪种方法，将取决于荷载是如何规定的。如果荷载随时间的变化是完全已知的，虽然它可以是高度变化不定的或者其性质是不规则变化的，我们将把它称为非随机动荷载；而任何特定的结构体系在非随机动荷载下的反应分析通常定义为确定分析。另一种情况，如果荷载随时间的变化不是完全已知的，但可从统计方面来进行定义，这种荷载则称为随机动荷载，而非确定分析对应于随机动荷载下的反应分析。本书的重点放在确定动力分析方法的叙述上。

一般来说，动力荷载下的结构反应主要是用结构的位移来表示的。因此，确定分析能导出相应于规定的荷载时程的位移-时间过程，结构的其他确定反应，如应力、应变、内力等等，通常作为分析的次要方面，可从前面所建立的位移模式求得。另一种情况是，非确定分析提供有关位移的统计资料，而这种位移是由统计定义的荷载所产生的。由于这时位移随时间的变化是不确定的，因而，其他的反应，如应力、内力等，必须用特定的非确定分析方法直接计算，而不是由所得位移来计算。

结构动力学问题在两个重要的方面不同于它的静荷载问题。第一个不同点，根据定义就是动力问题具有随时间而变化的性质。由于荷载和反应随时间而变化，显然动力问题不象静力问题那样具有单一的解，而必须建立相应于反应时程中感兴趣的全部时间的一系列解答。因此，动力分析显然要比静力分析更复杂且更花费时间。

但是，静力问题和动力问题还有更重要的区别，如在图 14-1 中所示那样（见阅读材料B）。如果一简支梁承受一静荷载 p，如图 14-1（a）所示，则它的弯矩、剪力及挠曲形状直接依赖于给定的荷载，而且可根据所建立的力的平衡原理用 p 求出。另一方面，如果荷载 $p(t)$ 是动力的，如图 14-1（b）所示，则所产生的梁的位移与加速度有联系，这些加速度又产生与其反向的惯性力。于是，在图 14-1（b）中梁的弯矩和剪力不仅要平衡外加荷载，而且要平衡由于梁的加速度所引起的惯性力。

以这样方式抵抗结构的加速度的惯性力是结构动力学问题的一个最重要的区别特征。一般来说，如果惯性力是结构内部弹性力所平衡的全部荷载中的一个重要部分，则在解题时必须考虑问题的动力特性。另一方面，如果运动是如此缓慢，以致惯性力小到可以忽略不计，则即使荷载和反应可能随时间变化，但对任何所需瞬时的分析，仍可用静力结构分析的方法来解决。

第15单元
弹性力学理论的内容

弹性力学理论，常简称为弹性力学，是固体力学的一个分支，它研究弹性固体中由于外力作用或温度变化而产生的应力和变形。

对不同工程学科的学生来说，学习弹性力学的目的意在分析弹性范围内各种结构或机械构件的应力和位移，校核它们是否具有所需的强度、刚度和稳定性。尽管研究弹性力学与研究材料力学和结构力学的目的相同，但是固体力学的这三个分支无论在研究对象上还是在分析方法上均互不相同。

材料力学主要研究结构或机械构件的应力和位移，这些构件常以直杆或曲杆的形状出现，并承受拉伸、压缩、剪切、弯曲和扭转等荷载的作用。建立在材料力学基础上的结构力学研究结构物的应力和位移，这种结构物常以杆件体系形式出现，如桁架或刚架。至于非杆件体系结构，如块、板、壳、堤坝、地基等实体结构则在弹性力学里进行研究，而为了全面、精确地分析杆状构件，也必须采用弹性力学理论。

虽然材料力学和弹性力学均研究杆状构件，但二者采用的分析方法不尽相同。材料力学研究承受外荷载的杆状构件时，往往对构件应变状态或应力分布作出假设，这就在一定程度上简化了数学推导，但常常不可避免地降低了所获结果的精确程度。然而在弹性力学中，对杆状构件研究往往不需要那些假设，因此，所得结果比较精确，并可用于校核材料力学里所得到的近似的解答。

例如，在材料力学中研究一个在横向荷载作用下直梁的弯曲问题时，就假定梁的平截面在弯曲后仍保持平面。这就导致横截面上的弯应力按直线分布。但在弹性力学理论里，不需引用这样假定同样可以解决类似问题，并能证明如果梁的高度并不远小于梁的跨度时，那么横截面上的弯应力远非直线分布，而且材料力学大大地低估了最大拉应力。

又例如，在材料力学里计算有孔的等截面拉伸构件的应力时，通常假定拉应力在净截面上均匀分布，然而弹性力学理论的精确分析表明净截面上的拉应力绝非均匀分布，而是集中在孔的附近，孔边缘的最大应力远远超过净截面上的平均应力。

在20世纪以前，杆件体的正式分析只出现在结构力学而不是弹性力学里。尽管此习惯仍然存在，但本世纪的许多工程师还是采用相互渗透的方法，综合应用固体力学中这两个学科的知识。结构力学中多种分析方法的应用大大增强了弹性力学的理论，因而使工程师们能获得弹性力学中许多复杂问题的解答。尽管这些解答在理论上有一定的近似性，但对工程设计来讲是有足够的精确度。例如，利用近30年发展起来的有限元法，我们可以先把要研究的物体离散化，然后采用结构力学里的位移法、力法或者混合法来解决弹性力学里的问题。这是固体力学中两个学科的综合运用的杰出例子。

此外，在进行结构设计时对该结构的各个构件，甚至对单一构件的不同部分可以采用固体力学中不同学科的方法，从而可以花费最小的工作量获得最满意的结果。

学生们不应当过多地考虑固体力学中这三门学科之间模糊的而且是暂时的分界线，相反，应引导他们去重视综合应用这三个学科知识的一切可能性。

第 16 单元

有限元法的发展史

有限元这一术语似乎是克拉夫在 1960 年发表的一篇文章里首创的新词。当时它是被用来描述分析弹性薄膜的一种计算方法，在这种计算方法中连续体被分为若干个离散的小而有限的子结构或单元。此观点并不新颖，事实上在 1949 年考伦特就提出过把连续体分成有限的部分，只不过随着数值计算的出现，此类计算法一直到 50 年代中期才得以实际应用。是特纳、克拉夫及其他人把离散元素的观点和用于矩阵结构分析的刚度法合二为一，创造了一个后来被称为有限元法的系统程序。在克拉夫本人对此阶段的评述中可以找到有关有限元早期发展的有趣记载。

在随后的年月里，有限元法得以迅速的普及。在此词诞生之后的 10 年里，千篇以上论及有限元的文章在一些科学文献里发表。20 年以后，在 COMPENDEX-PLUS 工程索引中列出的相关文章的数目达到 5 万篇。这个飞快发展的速度反映了有限元概念与数字计算机显示的计算能力的互补作用所达到的程度。最重要的是，有限元法使其自身投入到多功能程序的发展中。在 60 年代末期，有限元法导致了首批商业性有限元计算机编码的出现。这些编码是能够处理自然科学方面各种问题的程序，其方式是通过改变输入数据而不是改变编码本身。自那时起，这类程序在不断扩展，增多，现已包括一些工业标准程序：NASTRAN，ABAQUS，ADINA，ANSYS，PAFEC，SAP，MARC 和 EASE，仅举数例。最近又出现了适用于新一代个人计算机和调整代码的工作站程序，例如：MSC/PAL，ANSYS-PC，SAP90，COSMOS/M，ALGOR 等等。这些程序在应力分析方面的实际应用，已成为现代机械设计和结构设计主要进展之一。

另一个有助于 60 年代末以来有限元法迅速发展的因素是人们认识到此法还适用于固体和结构分析之外的问题。最初事实出现于齐安凯维兹和其他人的研究中，他们证明此法可以适用于包括拉普拉斯和波埃森方程在内的场问题（例如稳定热传导或者无粘性流体的位流）。60 年代初期，伴随这些新发展，又出现了新认识，即加辽金法和其他的加权残数技术可以用来作为一个理论根据证实有限元法能应用于实际上任何以偏微分方程形式出现的问题。结果，目前有限元法运用的领域包括流体力学，空气动力学，声学，润滑理论，地质力学，大气动力学，电磁理论等等。

如果只谈在固体和结构力学上的应用，到 60 年代有限元法已是非常先进的，它有能力解决线弹性范围内的二维或三维问题。但是它仍需要大量的计算——取决于当时一般的计算条件——并且有限元法只限于解决大规模的工业研究或者学术研究方面的问题。在此法的应用方面，一个新近最卓有成效的发展是促使计算的实际成本稳步降低，而不是方法本身的任何具体进展（新单元，新解法等等）。这使有限元计算成为工程设计的主要组成部分，工程师可通过手边的相对适当的计算设备利用有限元进行常规设计分析。许多商业程序在工程工作站或个人计算机里正有效地运行着，大量分析只需花费相当于 10 年前类似计算所需费用的一小部分。这预示着一个几年后工程技术领域更充分运用有限元法的趋势。

　　实际计算费用的持续降低——这一现象的一个附加作用产生于工程领域里计算机制图的使用，反过来又促进了计算机辅助设计和计算机辅助制造的发展。自从有限元计算模型的产生能够容易地与图形表示法结合以来，有限元法的实际应用一直在得到这些发展的推动，而这种图形表示法是处在计算机辅助设计及计算机辅助制造革命的中心位置。因此，当今几乎没有计算机辅助设计系统不能提供把图形信息与兼容的有限元程序互换的功能。图形设计（用计算机辅助设计系统）与定量分析（用有限元程序）的这种结合使有限元法的数据准备和有限元分析结果的显示，大体上说至少比六七十年代类似的有限元程序所耗用的时间少一个数量级。

Appendix III Key to Exercises

UNIT ONE
Reading comprehension
  I . 1. C   2. B   3. C   4. C   5. C
  II . 1. E   2. C   3. A   4. B   5. F   6. D
 III . 1. … axially-loaded bars, shafts, and columns, structures that are assemblies of these components
    2. … available to us ……
    3. … stress and strain.
    4. … the axial force P acts through …, … can be demonstrated by statics.
    5. … a tensile strain, … a compressive strain.

Vocabulary
  I . 1. C   2. B   3. A   4. D   5. C
  II . 1. d   2. e   3. b   4. a   5. c

UNIT TWO
Reading Comprehension
  I . 1. B.   2. A.   3. C.   4. C.   5. B.
  II . 1. B   2. E   3. A   4. D   5. C   6. F
 III . 1. are measured
    2. maximum value/ aluminium stress
    3. stress up
    4. steel /many aluminium /classified
    5. be obtained / in compression / the yield point / be established

Vocabulary
  I . 1. A   2. D   3. C   4. B   5. A
  II . 1. d   2. g   3. b   4. a   5. e

UNIT THREE
Reading Comprehension
  I . 1. A   2. B   3. C   4. D   5. A
  II . 1. C   2. A   3. B   4. E   5. D   6. F   7. G
 III . 1. may be imposed upon them

167

2. as in the design of satellite/ the feasibility/ success of the whole mission

3. 19th century/ indelible impression

4. the most fundamental subjects of

5. numerous problems

Vocabulary

I. 1. C 2. D 3. C 4. B 5. A

II. 1. c 2. d 3. f 4. a 5. b

UNIT FOUR
Reading Comprehension

I. 1. A 2. D 3. C 4. B 5. A

II. 1. C 2. D 3. B 4. F 5. G 8. E 9. H
10. A 11. J 14. L 15. K

III. 1. Finally, by adding the forces on the restrained structure

2. as a second step these inconsistencies or "errors" in the released structure

3. unlike the force method, with respect to the restraining forces

4. equal to the degree of indeterminacy. the removal of an external or an internal force

5. for a unit value of displacement

Vocabulary

I. 1. A 2. D 3. C 4. B 5. A

II. 1. g 2. a 3. e 4. b 5. f

UNIT FIVE
Reading Comprehension

I. 1. D 2. A 3. B 4. D 5. C

II. 1. G 2. A 3. J 4. D 5. C 6. F 7. K
8. E 9. B 10. L 11. I 12. H

III. 1. establish, reinforce, volumes, planes

2. 1)stability 2)strength and stiffness 3)economy

3. raw materials, fabrication, erection, maintenance.

4. in terms of

5. inherently, fireproofing materials

Vocabulary

    I. 1.B   2.B   3.A   4.D   5.C

    II. 1.b   2.d   3.f   4.g   5.e

UNIT SIX

Reading Comprehension

    I. 1.B   2.C   3.D   4.C   5.A

    II. 1.B   2.H   3.F   4.A   5.G   6.C   7.I   8.D   9.E

    III. 1. At this stage / loads / member properties

        2. For this reason / to a model which is susceptible

        3. An up-to-date /in the bases of matrix structural analysis / as well as in the use of available analysis

        4. it is necessary to start with / which can then be

        5. The modern matrix—computer methods / by making it possible to analyze entire systems / about the behavior of structures under loads

Vocabulary

    I. 1.A   2.B   3.D   4.B   5.C

    II. 1.c   2.a   3.e   4.b   5.f

UNIT SEVEN

Reading Comprehension

    I. 1.C   2.B   3.D   4.C   5.A

    II. 1.C   2.E   3.G   4.I   5.D   6.A   7.H   8.J   9.B   10.F

    III. 1. for handling and placing / to drop markedly

        2. formable / moldable

        3. The American Concrete Institute / reinforced concrete

        4. Modern transit—mixed concrete suppliers / uniformly high quality

        5. it can also serve as an effective barrier

Vocabulary

    I. 1.B   2.B   3.A   4.C   5.A

    II. 1.b   2.d   3.e   4.a   5.c

UNIT EIGHT

Reading Comprehension

I. 1. D 2. C 3. A 4. B 5. D

II. 1. D 2. G 3. E 4. C 5. B 6. H 7. F 8. A

III. 1. are concerned

2. meet the standard / have the authority to order

3. all constuuction be accomplished, specified materiacls, special way.

4. the performance standards of are outlined free to select building techniques.

5. free to/ plastic pipe/ cast-iron pipe/ gold pipe/ as long as

Vocabulary

I. 1. A 2. A 3. C 4. B 5. D

II. 1. a 2. c 3. e 4. d 5. b

UNIT NINE

Reading Comprehension

I. 1. C 2. D 3. B 4. D 5. D

II. 1. C 2. F 3. I 4. B 5. J 6. G 7. E 8. A 9. H 10. D

III. 1. rammed earth, stone blocks laid one on another without benefit of any bonding or cementing medium

2. soil or earth, the lime and the sand, cementing material

3. has the capability of hardening under water

4. 1) proportioning limestone and clay

   2) burning the mixture at a high temperature to produce clinkers

   3) then grinding the clinkers to produce a hydraulic cement

5. the quality of concrete is directly affected by the amount of water in relation to the amount of cement; within reasonable limits, the quality of the concrete decreases as the water-cement ratio goes up

Vocabulary

I. 1. B 2. D 3. A 4. D 5. D

II. 1. c 2. e 3. f 4. g 5. a

UNIT TEN
Reading Comprehension
　　Ⅰ. 1. D　2. C　3. D　4. B　5. D
　　Ⅱ. 1. B　2. J　3. G　4. I　5. D　6. A　7. C　8. E　9. H　10. F
　Ⅲ. 1. Portland cement, water, sand, crushed gravel, stone
　　　2. compressive strength, durability, tensile strength
　　　3. moisture, within, cold weather, may freeze, serious frost damage
　　　4. 4, 8 gal per sack of cement
　　　5. 6 gal, per sack, the maximum amount, less, stronger

Vocabulary
　　Ⅰ. 1. D　2. C　3. B　4. D　5. B
　　Ⅱ. 1. e　2. d　3. h　4. c　5. a

UNIT ELEVEN
Reading Comprehension
　　Ⅰ. 1. B　2. C　3. A　4. D　5. C
　　Ⅱ. 1. E　2. B　3. D　4. A　5. G　6. C　7. H　8. F
　Ⅲ. 1. mixture, a cementitious material, sand
　　　2. has set, are bound together, they form a single structure unit
　　　3. bind the masonry units together, resist comprehesive loads, add to the strength of the masonry units
　　　4. a seperation of the mortar from the brick
　　　5. trowel smoothly, evenly; without effort

Vocabulary
　　Ⅰ. 1. D　2. C　3. D　4. B　5. A
　　Ⅱ. 1. d　2. e　3. f　4. c　5. g

UNIT TWELVE
Reading Comprehension
　　Ⅰ. 1. B　2. D　3. C　4. C　5. A
　　Ⅱ. 1. C　2. B　3. I　4. A　5. D　6. E　7. F　8. G　9. H
　Ⅲ. 1. just one
　　　2. economic aspects, an architect
　　　3. coordination, the potential of achieving an economical solution

4. superstructure, substructure, soil

5. 1) energy supply system may be concentrated in mechanical cores

   2) separate duct spaces are provided in the exterior facade

   3) interspatial systems with mechanical levels used

Vocabulary

I. 1.D 2.B 3.A 4.C 5.A

II. 1.a 2.c 3.d 4.e 5.g

UNIT THIRTEEN

Reading Comprehension

I. 1.B 2.C 3.D 4.A 5.A

II. 1.C 2.A 3.G 4.D 5.F 6.E 7.H 8.B

III. 1. place bathrooms, windows,

2. corrugated, troughed, flat steel, plywood, aluminium, asestos-cement.

3. on the inner face, on the outer face.

4. polythene, metal, other material.

5. the walls of large precast concrete units

Vocabulary

I. 1.C 2.D 3.A 4.D 5.D

II. 1.d 2.b 3.e 4.a 5.c

UNIT FOURTEEN

Reading Comprehension

I. 1.D 2.C 3.B 4.B 5.A

II. 1.B 2.E 3.G 4.A 5.F 6.D 7.C

III. 1. be looked upon merely, a special form of dynamic loading

2. be defined simply, time-vary, the magnitude, direction or position varies with time

3. is expressed basically; the displacements of the structure

4. its static-loading counterpart, two important respects

5. a significant portion, the internal elastic forces of the structure, be accounted for

Vocabulary

I. 1.D 2.B 3.B 4.C 5.A

II. 1.d 2.e 3.f 4.b 5.a

UNIT FIFTEEN

Reading Comprehension

    I. 1. C 2. D 3. B 4. A 5. C

    II. 1. C 2. A 3. G 4. E 5. B 6. I 7. F 8. H 9. D

    III. 1. stresses and deformations, external forces; changes in temperature

        2. blocks, plates, shells, dams and foundations

        3. more accurate, to check the approximate results, mechanics of materials

        4. 1) the discretization of the body concerned

           2) the application of the displacement method

           3) the force method

           4) the mixed method in structural mechanics

        5. the different branches; different members, different parts

Vocabulary

    I. 1. A 2. D 3. B 4. A 5. C

    II. 1. b 2. g 3. f 4. e 5. c

UNIT SIXTEEN

Reading Comprehension

    I. 1. C 2. A 3. D 4. B 5. D

    II. 1. B 2. D 3. A 4. E 5. C

    III. 1. a computational approach; elastic membranes

        2. discrete elements, stiffness approach, finite element method

        3. a theoretical basis, finite elements, partial differential equations

        4. 1) fluid mechanics

           2) aerodynamics

           3) acoustics

           4) lubrication theory

           5) geomechanics

           6) atmospheric dynamics

           7) electromagnetic theory

        5. finite element models; the geometric modelling techniques

Vocabulary

    I. 1. B 2. A 3. D 4. D 5. C

    II. 1. c 2. a 3. e 4. f 5. g

图书在版编目（CIP）数据

建筑类专业英语．建筑工程．第一册/卢世伟，孟祥杰主编．—北京：中国建筑工业出版社，1997（2005重印）
高等学校试用教材
ISBN 978-7-112-03029-3

Ⅰ．建…　Ⅱ．①卢…②孟…　Ⅲ．①建筑学-英语-高等学校-教材②建筑工程-英语-高等学校-教材　Ⅳ．H31

中国版本图书馆CIP数据核字（2005）第090442号

本书即《建筑类专业英语　工业与民用建筑》第一册，系根据国家教委印发的《大学英语专业阅读阶段教学基本要求》编写的。内容包括：材料力学、结构力学、结构动力学、弹性力学、结构分析、结构材料的特性、混凝土、砂浆、房屋建筑学、有限元法等。全书安排16个单元，每个单元除正课文外，还配有两篇阅读材料，并配有必要的注释。正课文还配有词汇表和练习，书后附有总词汇表、参考译文和练习答案。本书供建筑工程专业学生使用，也可供土建人员自学专业英语之用。

高等学校试用教材

建 筑 类 专 业 英 语

建筑工程

第一册

卢世伟　孟祥杰　　　　主编
史冰岩　齐秀坤　李　飓
李晶纯　南敬石　屠永清　黄　红　　编
刘建理　　　　　　　　　主审

*

中国建筑工业出版社出版、发行（北京西郊百万庄）
各地新华书店、建筑书店经销
廊坊市海涛印刷有限公司印刷

*

开本：787×1092毫米　1/16　印张：11¼　字数：274千字
1997年5月第一版　2017年1月第二十七次印刷
定价：20.00元
ISBN 978-7-112-03029-3
（20774）

版权所有　翻印必究
如有印装质量问题，可寄本社退换
（邮政编码 100037）